Marked Fo

Hope you enjoy!

Much love

Bill

To my 'elder' sister!

Some of this will help you catch up with what went on when you were in 'darkest Africa'!

Marked For Life

"The marks
of a man...

———

...who has met
with God."

Bill Davidson

Outskirts Press, Inc.
Denver, Colorado

Outskirts Press, Inc.
http://www.outskirtspress.com

ISBN: 9978-1-4327-4955-2

Outskirts Press and the "OP" logo are trademarks belonging to Outskirts Press, Inc.

We stand on the shoulders of so many who have touched our lives along the way. When writing a book containing biographical illustrations, the question is, which names to mention and which to leave out? I came to the conclusion that where necessary I would add a name or two, but for the most part very few pages contain the identities of my friends and colleagues to whom I owe so much. At the risk of offending a few, this is the route I have chosen.

No one will be offended, however, when I dedicate this little book to Jeanie - who from the moment I saw her at age fourteen, captured my heart – and to my 'kids'; Kellie and Craig - who had no choice but to accompany us on our life's adventures, but did so like the pioneers they are today – and to Jongie; that cheeky little boy in la Rosa de Saron children's home in Bogotá who stole our hearts and decided never to give them back.

Table of Contents

Chapter 1   Marked for Life 1

Chapter 2   Catching Thrown Stones 7

Chapter 3   Walking with a Limp 13

Chapter 4   Knowing Who You're Not! 23

Chapter 5   Ears Pierced 39

Chapter 6   The Greatest and the Least Important 61

Chapter 7   Directionally Challenged 69

Chapter 8   Dumb and Loving It! 85

Chapter 9   Getting Smaller Every Day 99

Chapter 10   On Crutches 109

Chapter 11   And in the End...Success 119

1

Marked for Life

I am convinced of this; God has a sense of humor! His dealings with humans could not be tolerated by a deity with anything less than a lively wit. I know full well that He is saddened by those who are lost. The Father claims His heart is "filled with pain"[1] over those who don't know Him, or His Son, who is the Way (and if you don't know the way, you're lost). But His relationship with His people, those who claim to be within His family, must surely cause a smile or two to emanate from the Heavenlies, if not a roar of laughter now and then.

My life and ministry have been marked by everything from profound remorse, deep sadness, joy, elation, fulfillment, then all the way through to the hilarious and a lot more that fits in somewhere between. It does sound a bit like blowing one's own trumpet – you'll have to be the judge of that as you read these pages – but God has allowed me some experiences, some marks along the way, which can only be described as extreme and extraordinary. And my soul bears these marks that testify to every step… sure or faltering.

---

1   Genesis 6:6 NIV

Nowadays, I look at the man in the mirror and see not so much a face, but more a road map. Marks have appeared that were not there some years before - marks that bear witness to events and circumstances through which I've walked. Others simply stand as testimony to the passage of time!

I carry blemishes, which have been around for quite a while; some longer than others. A mark in my forehead reminds me that despite my mother's warning, I couldn't keep from picking at least one of my chicken pox spots. A long scar under my arm recalls a brush with what some thought might be cancer, but the surgeon's scalpel betrayed the work of a Brown Recluse Spider which had probably made its home in my horse's hay bail. A plunge of my hand into that sweet smelling feed and I, unwittingly, became dinner for this tiny intruder. My knees and shins have marks that testify to participation in competitive soccer on frost hardened English, Italian and American fields, stretching over six decades from the 1950s into the new Millennium. Marked or not, some of us just don't know when to quit!

Most people I know who have been in ministry for any length of time carry the marks to prove it. I wish they were all laugh-lines! They appear as silent witnesses to a story, a drama. Soldiers carry their marks as badges of merit - scars that tell a thousand tales - but Christian soldiers are not so forthcoming with their wounds. Perhaps that's because ministry marks are mostly internal. Too often these wounds carry with them a sense of shame or regret. All too many were inflicted, you see, by "friendly fire".

If someone asks him, `What are these wounds on your body?'
He will answer, `The wounds I was given at the house of my friends.' [2]

In *Romeo & Juliet*, Shakespeare wrote: "He jests at scars who never felt a wound." [3] Few in ministry make such jests.

2   Zechariah 13:6 NIV
3   'Romeo & Juliet' Act II Prologue, Scene 1:43 William Shakespeare

J. Ray, a 17th Century writer, wrote in a book of English Proverbs: *"Wars bring scars."* Consequently, many are the marks of a man or woman in ministry.

Back in 1561, Pastor Guido de Bres, one of the leaders of the Reformation in the Low Countries of Western Europe, [4] penned a *Confession of Faith* that listed several distinguishable *Marks of a Christian*. They were: faith, the avoidance of sin, following after righteousness, love for God and for one's neighbor, and lastly (but seemingly not least) the crucifying of the flesh. These, he said, are the ultimate marks of a person who has met with God. They show all who care to see that the Father's fingerprint has been left on that life.

In his book, "The Marks of a Christian", Francis Schaeffer begins: *"Through the centuries men have displayed many different symbols to show that they are Christians. They have worn marks in the lapels of their coats, hung chains about their necks, even had special haircuts."* He goes on to speak of the inner work of love, the true mark of a Christian. [5]

However, there are other marks, wounds and scars, lines of concern and wrinkles of laughter. These mark the faces and the hearts of God's agents on Earth. Among these marks are some that distinguish the person as having actually met with God in a personal and intimate way. There is a difference, you see, between being marked by working *for* God and being marked by meeting *with* Him!

Those who merely work *for* God repeat His promises and gather supporters. They gain a following and see great things take place. *"Many will say to me on that day, `Lord, Lord, did we not prophesy in your name and in your name drive out demons and perform*

---

4   The region around modern Holland and Belgium
5   John 13:33-35

many miracles?" [6] Amazingly some of these people find the ability to glide through life without much persecution or opposition. Not many marks!

There are others, however, who have taken a different path, whether by their choosing or by God's design – hopefully both. They take the path our forebears called 'the way of the cross'. These are the men and women who, along the way, genuinely met with God. For them *the things of earth have grown strangely dim in the light of His glory and grace.* [7] Like Paul, they say: *"I consider that our present sufferings are not worth comparing with the glory that will be revealed in us."* [8]

So, what are the authentic marks of these people? Are there some common signs that testify to their encounter with The Almighty? If there are, shouldn't we be eager to identify them? Isn't our generation characterized by a desire to follow those who have been "in the Presence" - those who have "the anointing"?

The Bible makes it clear that the marks of a person who has met with God are not always those we might expect or even desire. To the undiscerning eye, the marks of a person who has encountered the Almighty can sometimes look more like those of a person who has recently met with disaster!

One thing is sure: God's marks on a person will seldom be confused with the world's marks of success. What we commonly associate with the mark of an anointed ministry is sometimes quite contrary to the genuine mark of God's approval. Too often the mark of a modern ministry is associated more with a person's following and popularity than with his character or relationship with God.

---

6   Matthew 7:22,23 NIV
7   'Turn Your Eyes Upon Jesus' – Helen H. Lemmel, 1922
8   Romans 8:18 NIV

So, let's discover together the genuine marks of a person who has met with God and yet lived to tell the tale. Let's ask God what His badges of merit really look like – and feel like. Instead of being things which we think we would desire and for which we would work hard to achieve, some of these distinguishing marks will hold little attraction to us while others are more obvious signs of blessing. I think we'll discover that only a few of them are found on the mountain top. They are not Olympic Gold. More often than not, they appear at the far end of valleys. The recipients always know they have been honored by the award, but others might look on and see only what appears to be continuing failure.

People spoken of in the Bible, who bore such marks, are described in Hebrews 11:38. Rather than featuring prominently in present-day Christian magazines or talk shows, they might be assigned to the category of being "under the dealings of God," or worse, "Under attack from the enemy"! The truth is they bore in their bodies the marks of what it really means to be a man or woman of God. The writer of Hebrews calls them those *"Of whom the world was not worthy."*

As these pages will reveal, God's marks on my life range from the downright hilarious, through the truly remarkable and on into those unforgettable touches from His hand which formed what is now my character. That's it, in a nutshell. The mark of a person who has had an encounter with God is *'Character'*. Not giftedness – just Character. I have my share of gifts, as we all do. I am aware of them and have tried to hone them to a reasonable degree. But the bottom line of our walk with God is measured by the degree to which we have allowed Him to shape us. Godly character is evidence of our obedient response to His touch, His word, His commands - His significant mark upon a human heart.

2
Catching Thrown Stones

I entered the hospital in Tel Aviv with two concerns. The first was that I had gone deaf in my left ear. It was no big deal, really. A few days before arriving in Israel, I had been playing my very first game of American Football on a beach on the Mediterranean island of Crete. In the process of my initiation into this great game I ended up several times with my British face in the sand. Consequently, I came away carrying a considerable portion of Crete in my hearing system. That was my first concern – and my least. My second was that I had not one shekel, penny, or cent to pay for any treatment I might be afforded. Israel, I had been told, was a very expensive place to be in need of medical attention, or anything else, for that matter!

You may ask how a man, at that time residing in the UK, could be traveling through the Middle East without any money! Well, I was in Youth With A Mission, and if you know anything about YWAM and YWAMers, and their seemingly unlimited ability to traverse the high-wire of international travel without any visible means of support, then, *"Nuff said!"*

My translator explained my physical condition to the doctor on duty who then proceeded to flush most of Crete out of my head and into a stainless steel tureen. So far, so good! Now at least I would be able to hear him tell me how much I owed the hospital for the favor!

The Doctor started writing my bill. "His name?" He asked, in Hebrew. The translator said, in English, "Davidson". Not easy in Hebrew it would seem. "Day – veee – zohn" the Doctor attempted, then tried to write it down. "No" my friend continued in Hebrew. "Ben David" – (Son of David). The doctor looked at me, crumpled my bill in his hand and said; "Son of David!? Hah! He pays nothing here!" And out we walked.

I did not linger to clarify the fact that my *"King David"* had been a war-painted Celtic pagan who spent most of his time chopping up the English over two thousand years after the famed King of Israel had served the purposes of God in his generation and fallen asleep. [9] It seemed prudent at the time to accept my new identity, if only for the sake of the economy, and beat a hasty retreat.

That is about as close as I have come to a practical association with the biblical King David, except for the fact that the description of his life in the narrative of the Prophet Samuel and the expression of his heart in his many Psalms, shows him to be a man above all other biblical characters with whom I can identify.

David was a man marked by the varying circumstances of his long and active life. Even before he was out of his teens his arms must have been scarred by the claw of the bear and the lion,[10] but his greatest marks were those impressed within him by the finger of God and usually after times when David had well and truly blown it!

---

9   Acts 13:36
10   1 Samuel 17:36

There are many stories that characterize David as a remarkable man. How about the time when he had a craving for a good long drink from the well in Bethlehem, which, at the time, was under Philistine hands. Three men broke through the enemy's lines, drew water and brought it back to their leader. Such was the devotion he inspired in them! Seeing their bravery, David declared that he was not worthy of such commitment, and poured out the water on the ground. [11]

That was quite a man and quite a leader! However, I wonder whether most of us would not be able to rise to such integrity given that kind of devotion and support from our followers. Even I have been known to be quite noble when supported by a crowd and as the recipient of a deep level of commitment. My tests have usually come when my soldiers have fallen out of line or joined another battalion leaving their beloved leader to tap his own drum and keep in step with his own penny-whistle! At times like these (and they come to most leaders in just about every field) my attitude has occasionally been far less noble or leader-like.

David passed that test also. And this marks him out as having the true badge of a man who has met with God and allowed His divine imprint to remain on his life.

One of the most amazing stories in David's life came when his own son, Absalom, rebelled against his kingship. Cleverly, he stole the hearts of the people from his father and eventually took over the throne, leaving David, the great king, to flee from Jerusalem. [12]

Imagine the sense of shame and bitter disappointment that clouded the flight of David and those who were with him. These were the soldiers who had been known as David's Mighty Men of Valor. Now they were a disorganized rabble of middle-aged men fleeing behind their disenfranchised leader.

11   2 Samuel 23:15-17
12   2 Samuel 15:13

To make matters worse, on their way out of office, they passed the house of a family member of King Saul, who was no doubt still sore at the up-start David taking what he saw as his family's place in history. Emboldened by David's shameful retreat, the man ran from his house and picked up stones and threw them at the king, in the same way he might drive off a bothersome dog from his front porch! *"Get out, get out, you man of bloodshed and worthless fellow,"* he yelled.[13] Stones scattered around the feet of the monarch of Israel and no doubt pinged off the armor of his entourage. This was too much for Abishai who walked beside the king. He was all for cutting off the head of this "dead dog".

It was then that David showed a characteristic to which men never attain by any other course but by having been under the dealings of God. He replied to Abishai; *"Behold, my son who came out from me seeks my life; how much more now this Benjamite? Let him alone and let him curse, for the LORD has told him. Perhaps the LORD will look on my affliction and return good to me instead of his cursing this day."* [14]

David showed the mark of a man who has met with God; namely, his ability to catch throne stones. Let me explain......

Have you ever heard the phrase used in wartime, "There's a bullet out there with your name on it"? This inspired the writers of the British comedy series *"Black Adder"* to show Baldrick, a British soldier in the trenches during the First World War, scratching his name on a bullet. "If there is a bullet with my name on it," he reasoned, "I thought it would be much safer in my pocket!

In a similar way, there are stones out there, flying around in the air of our battles – and not all are hurled by the enemy. Some hit us on the back of the head, and we are left to wonder which one of our regiment threw them!

---

13   2 Samuel 16
14   Verse 11

However, maturity is not simply learning the ability to stand in the midst of the stone throwing or even how to retreat with dignity! The real mark of a man who has been through God's dealings is to find strength enough to catch the stone and see if his name is on it. In other words, to say, *"Lord, however unjust this stone throwing might be, is there something I need to learn from it? Are you speaking to me?"*

When criticized, the best response of a man of God will not be to hurl a few stones back, in order to even things up a bit, but rather to ask God if He would prefer to use this situation to teach him something about himself.

To be truthful, I have seldom been criticized or opposed without providing at least some basis for the frustration or disappointment which provoked the criticism. So perhaps God has as many opportunities to work in us when we are wrong as He might have when we are right!

It is significant to me that just prior to founding Church of The King here in Queensbury, New York [15] I went through one of the darkest times of my life. Hurt and confused, feeling betrayed and rejected, I lashed out a few times in attempts to justify my 'righteous' position. It was then God convinced me that if I handed the mess over to Him, together with the bitterness which so easily overran my heart, all would be well — or even better than 'well'. Somehow that awful season led directly into my relationship with my band of brothers throughout the world in Alliance International Ministries and the best times of our lives. [16]

David knew this principle. He had been humbled by his own weakness. He had often placed his hand in the undoing of other men's lives. He had known what it was to trade his godly jealousy for the cheaper commodity which cares first for the stuff of position and personal power.

---

15   For online reference, see: "cotk.net"
16   For online reference see: "aimteam.org"

Anyone who has ever lost something dear to himself; a marriage, a ministry, a position, a standing among his peers, will know the sense of bereavement which dogs the night hours and clouds the days. Stepping down from the throne of his unfulfilled expectations is a man's most difficult move. And to make matters worse, the road that leads out of the city of one's dreams into the desert of one's realities is often peopled with stone throwers who once were called friends.

There is a way back. Even before we have to deal with forgiveness, reconciliation, restoration, and all that might one day see us restored to our place of influence and fulfillment, there is a first step. Catch that stone! Turn it over and see if your name is there. And even if you never regain your throne – even if you are to be locked out of the city – even if, for the rest of your life, the stone-throwers believe the lie – you will still have grown where it matters.

You will have learned that God is more motivated by your character than by your popularity and more concerned with your destination than with the transport by which you arrive. God will have looked into your heart and found that you are more concerned with learning your lesson than proving your point. The days of sorrow and seeming defeat will have been miraculously reversed into the finest hours of your life, because through them, you came to bear a mark of a man who has met with God.

3

Walking with a Limp

When friends first came to visit us in our first Adirondack [17] home, I admit I would boast a little, recounting – with humble dignity, of course - the stories, of how we had walked onto a ten acre piece of northern forest and declared "this is the place". We knew it was the plot, just around the corner from our Church building, on which we would build our family home.

To get the full impact of our challenge, you must understand that this was not exactly a city building lot, with gas, electricity, sewers and water already laid on. This was the Adirondacks! Critters, rocks and trees! More rocks than critters and more trees than rocks.

A few years earlier, my wife Jean and I had migrated with our young kids from the UK. I had little more than a screw driver in my tool chest. To be truthful, that tool chest was metaphorical, and my screw driver would have tested me to know which end to hold. The months that lay ahead turned me, by necessity, into a true

---

17   The Adirondack Mountains of Upstate New York

Adirondack man, complete with chain saw, work clothes, boots, flannel shirt – the whole kit and caboodle!

Ed Winslow and Skip Sanders were my mentors. Patiently, they went about their business of clearing the tall pines, pulling the stumps and skidding the logs. I followed behind and did what I was told. In time I learned how to cut my wedge and fell even the biggest meanest trees just about exactly where they should fall – a critical issue at times. It was without doubt the hardest work this man could dream of (even on a very bad night). Every evening saw me more and more convinced of how it must have felt for my ancestors, toiling all day in pitch battle with nothing but an ox in one hand and a Celtic broad-sword in the other. To me, that's how logging with a chain saw felt in the mid summer heat.

I mentioned to Skip how it must have been in earlier times for the pioneers who broke ground in this area of New York, which to the people of New England was 'the frontier'. They didn't have chains saws, skidders, back-hoe, dozer and chains. A settler might have had the help of his wife and small daughter, and maybe an ox or a mule to help pull the stumps. "But just remember" said Skip. "We're dealing with seventy year-old trees because all this used to be grazing land for sheep. Back then they were dealing with trees that had stood for a thousand years!" Point taken!

Eventually, it was done; the land was cleared, the hole was dug, the slab put down and the basement walls erected. Louis Miller, a skilled Mennonite builder, became my next teacher. He set about his trade in a way that awed me. I learned something new every day – every hour. I was really growing in my knowledge. "Tradesmen's secrets" I realized were only secrets until the trades-man told someone else, and I was learning from the best.

Can you imagine what it was like to see our family actually move into that house? To enjoy our kids growing through their teens in our great "homestead" which had once been a wild forest of pines?

I often caught myself in amazement as I stepped out onto the large back deck to breathe the clean mountain air and cast my eyes toward the hills and the trees that surrounded us on every side. I had cleared all the messy Northern Pines away which cascade tons of acidic pine needles on any attempt at a lawn or a garden and generally look scraggly in the process. This allowed the hardwoods to flourish, especially the maples that turn in the Fall from fresh green to every shade between lemon yellow to deep gold and dark red. There are days at that time of the year when the evening sun will reflect down across the trees and turn the air to gold.

The Adirondack Region is a beautiful area. A friend once said that it must have been God, who directed us here. "First" he said, "had it not been God, you wouldn't have been able to find it." It is pretty remote, to city people. "And secondly," he continued, "had it not been God's guidance it would be a sin to live somewhere so beautiful!"

The Adirondacks is not only a beautiful region, it is also a very independent place, full of self-sufficient people. The very name Adirondack, given to this New York mountain range, means "bark eater", coming from the days when the Iroquois nations roamed the area, fishing what we now call the Hudson River and hunting the plateau that English Quakers named as Queensbury and Glens Falls. In Iroquois days when the cruel arctic winter took hold, drifting the snow above the head of any man, the softer "snow birds" fled south - into what we now call The Bible Belt! - but the hardened warriors stayed around, even if the bark on the trees was all they had for nourishment!

The locals haven't changed much. Self sufficient people seldom do. Anyone who clears the forest and puts up his family home is prone to pride rather than given to gratitude.

It's rather like the old gardener in England, who had raised a prize profusion of fruits, vegetables and flowers, the like of which only an Englishman has ever seen. The local pastor walked by one day and leaned over the wall in the hopes of engaging the old timer, who was not exactly a committed churchgoer, in conversation. "God has blessed you with a lovely garden, Joe." He said. "You reckon?" replied the old man. "You should have seen it before I came along, when God had it all to himself!"

It is his type that migrated to the Adirondacks! And, come to think of it, they lived in Israel too.

The Lord God was so faithful to His people, Israel, bringing them out of slavery and giving them everything upon which a good life depends. But His concern that they were an independent and self-sufficient bunch (just like the rest of us) was not misguided. He told them: *"When you have eaten and are satisfied, you shall bless the LORD your God for the good land which He has given you. "Beware lest you forget the LORD your God by not keeping His commandments and His ordinances and His statutes which I am commanding you today; lest, when you have eaten and are satisfied, and have built good houses and lived in them, and when your herds and your flocks multiply, and your silver and gold multiply, and all that you have multiplies, then your heart becomes proud, and you forget the LORD your God who brought you out from the land of Egypt, out of the house of slavery.* [18]

Independence and self-sufficiency – the hallmarks of all that is best and worst about western culture – is cursed with the potential that encourages many of us to assess our success as having come by the sweat of our brow and the strength of our own hands or the gifts we posses – as if they were of our own invention. All too few realize that not one brick would stand upon another; not one two-by-four would stay nailed in place, and not one gifting would be expressed but by the grace and mercy of its Maker

---

18   Deuteronomy 8:10-14 NAS

As a child I attended Sunday School in The Salvation Army. To accompany our singing we had our very own brass band, complete with drums booming and every kid in the place clapping and stamping their feet. We would sing great war-like songs, such as:

> Dare to be a Daniel,
> Dare to stand alone,
> Dare to have a purpose, firm,
> And dare to make it known. [19]

Just like Daniel there have been times when it seemed my wife and I have stood alone. Times when it seemed all Hell had aimed its fury on our ministry. In the late 1980s, our ministry went through a season of crisis, or should I say 'crises'. They all lined up and came together as if orchestrated by some unfriendly finger of fate.

We had recently commissioned a new "church plant", sending out several dozens of our best members from our original New York church plant, Church of The Nations in Lake Luzerne, along with several established leaders. They were to begin a work in the lovely city of Saratoga Springs, NY. Saratoga is a sophisticated stylish community, graced during the summer by the New York City Ballet Company and the Philadelphia Orchestra. The Vanderbilt Whitneys of this world call Saratoga 'home', especially during the Polo and horse racing season and top names in entertainment visit the stage of the Performing Arts Center (SPAC). You get the picture!

The church started well and continues to this day as one of the largest worshipping congregations in our region, but not all went well as a result of this step of faith. Back in the home church one leader expressed disagreement with the choice of the new church's leadership. He was an older man whom I respected very highly, and do so to this day, but I backed the young pastor of the new church. To our great disappointment, the older man resigned

19   'Dare to be a Daniel' - by Philip Bliss

from his position of eldership and left our church, unintentionally attracting a large group of members to follow suit. Two other leaders were walking through a period of personal adjustment and had to resign from their responsibilities, leaving only two of us out of the original team. This caused no end of turmoil in the membership of the church, and I seemed to have little ability to effectively turn their hearts toward the positive.

As you can imagine I spent much time seeking God in all of this and one thought repeatedly came to my mind. We had to decide whether or not we were a true church, with the ability to weather such a stormy season, or were we merely a group of people who attended meetings together. (Not a bad question to put to any church, in any season).

To this end, I stood before our people and declared a two month pause from all organized Church activity. No Sunday or weekday meetings. "We'll come back on the first Sunday in October," I said; that being two months ahead. "And if it's just Jean and me and the kids, well, so be it. We'll start again." It would not be the first time our family had stood alone to pioneer a work, and might not be the last. We were ready, if necessary to 'dare to stand alone'.

I hasten to add that we were not left alone. The Church rose up and lived again, on into its greatest years. Church planters, like the apostles of old, must be prepared to take the risky step of standing apart from the crowd. The problem is we often face that challenge with the determination of our own will and from the pit of our courage, rather than by God's sustaining grace.

Whether you are setting up a ministry, building a house, caring for a loved one, raising the kids in a one-parent home, or pushing on through where others have feared to tread, it is all too easy to stand out on the back porch of our lives and say "by the sweat of my brow and by the strength of my hand, I have done this thing."

Admirable as self-sufficiency might appear, every inch of our independence prevents a mile of God's grace and, somehow, God's great love must work in us gently but firmly to shake that godless independence from our frame.

Such a shaking took place one night on the banks of the River Jordan. God told Jacob to go back home and face his brother Esau. That doesn't sound too much of a challenge until you recall that the last time the two boys had cohabited, Jacob had lived up to his name which means "heal catcher" or literally, *supplanter*.[20] He had used trickery and deceit to fool his earthy brother out of his inheritance and the 'blessing of the first born' which was Esau's birthright. Now, God told him, it was time to go back home to Esau and face the music.[21]

As Jacob approached the region of his home the Bible tells us he sent his belongings and his wives on ahead of him while he hung back on the banks of the river. [22] No doubt he was concerned as to the reception he was about to get. He didn't yet know the story of the Prodigal Son where the returning son was received by his father who *"fell on his neck and kissed him"* [23] Jacob was fully expecting someone to fall on his neck, but not with kisses!

It was at this point – when Jacob seemed ready to reconsider his life of trickery and independent self-promotion – that God arranged for Jacob to have one of those in-your-face encounters which we men least expect, and God most enjoys. It took the form of a wrestling match; a bout that would leave its mark on Jacob, for life.

It isn't clear who the 'man' was whom Jacob wrestled with that night on the river bank, but clearly Jacob saw it as nothing less than a

---

20   Strong's Words # 6117
21   Genesis 32:9
22   Genesis 32
23   Luke 15:20

meeting with God. [24] He named the place *Peniy-el*, or 'face of God'. He believed he had seen God and lived to tell the story.

The 'man' seemed to bear out Jacob's sense of a Divine encounter by renaming Jacob. *"Your name will no longer be Jacob,"* He said, *'but Israel, because you have struggled with God and with men and have overcome."* [25] During that famous bout, Jacob received an injury. His hip was put out of joint; so much so that he walked thereafter with a limp. To this day, every Jewish family remembers that night – and that fight. [26] The night God crippled one of the Patriarchs!

But why on earth would God do such a thing? Perhaps it was to leave a mark and a memorial to Jacob and to successive generations by putting to death a proud man's independence. Never again would Jacob take a step without a limp. Wherever he went from that day forward each step of the way would remind him that the next step is only by God's grace and did not come from his own strength and ability.

Perhaps a preacher should 'limp' to the pulpit. A prophet should 'limp' before opening his mouth. A 'signs and wonders' evangelist should 'limp' before the excited crowds, because it's all too easy to exchange the limp of God's dealings – the mark of God's making – for the swagger of man's abilities.

The Apostle Paul once wrote: *Even if I should choose to boast, I would not be a fool, because I would be speaking the truth. But I refrain, so no one will think more of me than is warranted by what I do or say. To keep me from becoming conceited because of these surpassingly great revelations, there was given me a thorn in my flesh, a messenger of Satan, to torment me.*[27]

---

24   Genesis 32:30
25   Genesis 32:29
26   Genesis 32:32
27   2 Corinthians 12:6,7

We have all heard a ton of my fellow preachers attempting to translate Paul's "thorn in the flesh". Some say it was a physical ailment. Some have even suggested it might have been an unbelieving wife who left him at the time of his conversion. I have lightheartedly considered the joke being on us all when we find out one day that his 'thorn in the flesh' was actually … a thorn in the flesh! (the last thing we preachers would think of!)

One thing is sure; Jacob's "thorn" was Jacob's limp! It was there as a perpetual reminder that the next step – the next breath – the next miracle – the next revelation, was by God's grace and not by his own ability.

We would do well to request from God that he marks us with a limp or two, along our way, just to make sure that on that great and awesome day when we meet with God we have the privilege of limping into His presence as humbled servants. There is an alternative: it is running unhindered into the desert of His absence.

Visiting Winkey Pratney back in the 1970s he suggested to me that I might like to accompany him to a small Texas church to hear a young singer who he believed was going to make a big splash one day. We turned up before the concert was about to begin. A lone grand piano and a single microphone stood waiting on stage. Winkey and I were ushered into a back room where we found the young singer. He was praying. The first thing I noticed was his shock of dark curly hair and his blue dungarees – giving him the appearance of a young David, who had decided against kingship and had taken up picking cotton.

We prayed together and then the young man stretched himself out on the floor, face down. "Oh God" he cried out. "If you don't go out there with me I have nothing to give."

A few minutes later Keith Green did go out there and gave expression to his amazing talent which a short time later was enjoyed for only too brief a period by the world. His talent could have taken him anywhere. I remember those great songs; the profound lyrical and musical artistry. But what I most recall is what I saw in that back room of a Texas church; Keith chose to walk with a limp.

4

Knowing Who You're Not!

In his book, *"The Body"*, Charles Colson writes: *The gospel teaches that our hope is not finding our true self, but losing our true self. That which defiles us is that which is in us, Christ said. When we honestly look inside at our sin-scarred lives, we ought to be repulsed by our "true" selves. We then repent and die to ourselves so that Christ's atoning grace might cleanse us.*[28]

We have the strangest ways of trying to define just who we are. It is part of the process of our "growing up"; a process most women seem to master (or should that be *"mistress"*) some time before the males of the species begin to get the idea.

Part of our search for identity involves us playing seasonal pretend games. Sadly, for all too many men and their longsuffering wives, the games continue well into adulthood. The motivation behind many an executive, politician, or even a famous preacher or two, has been a search for identity through fame, ability, power and popularity.

---

28   *The Body* by Charles Colson – © 1992 WORD Publishing – page 45

It all started innocently enough. I remember sneaking into the cinema in Cherry Lane in the Anfield district of Liverpool. Actually, 'sneaking' was all any good Salvation Army boy could do into such a place of worldly entertainment – so I snook - and there, up on the screen, in living black and white, I saw a teenage Elvis Presley.

We pre-Beatle Liverpudlians couldn't understand a word of the dialogue. Memphis and the mean streets of Liverpool were culturally as far apart as Memphis and the moon. He could have been singing in tongues for all we knew. Not that it mattered. Every time Elvis opened his mouth the girls who were present screamed so loud we couldn't hear him anyway. But somehow, something communicated to me and to an entire generation.

I emerged from the movie a new man – all 14 years of me. My walk assumed a somewhat freer swing to every stride. I was moving – I assured myself – just like Elvis.

Passing ladies hurriedly shoved their push-chaired kids through the puddles and onward to the corner shops, but I was walking through another place. A free-ranging lip curling, word-slurring place where Elvis lived and walked as no other mortal walked. No doubt had the passing shoppers cast a glance in my direction, they might have thought I was recovering from a bout of Polio, or that at least that I was wearing ill-fitting shoes. But I was secure – for the time being – in my new identity!

Such silliness can be excused in childhood. Just as excuses can be made for the hours I spent singing into my hair brush microphone using my bedroom mirror as my own private all-in-one TV camera and screen.

"When I was a child," Paul wrote. *"I talked like a child, I thought like a child, I reasoned like a child. When I became a man, I put*

childish ways behind me. [29] Ah, there's the rub. It's the putting away of childish things that proves difficult, especially in the pursuit of finding ones real identity which – in childhood – is so often rooted in foolishness.[30]

Four short years after my exposure to Elvis I left home to enter College. Now, I thought, I would soon discover who I really was. I knew I came from a home with a strong family identity. We were Christians, Salvationists, Scots, hopefully in that order. We were all musical. Whenever I left my house as a boy, the last thing I would hear as I swung the door closed was my Dad's voice, shouting from somewhere deep in the house: "Remember who you belong to!" I had my family identity. But who was "I", the "me" inside?

This question became extraordinarily important early in my College days as I embarked on the kind of experience of which most kids would only dream. I was about to become famous, recognized, popular, paid attention to, respected, applauded, even catered to, to an inordinate degree. So wouldn't this grant me a greater sense of identity? The fact is, it made it all the harder to know myself.

Let me tell you the story, as it happened...

I entered the William Booth College in London in the Fall of 1963. It was a vibrant place. Salvationist young people, for the most part, are fun-loving, motivated, and musical and the atmosphere seemed tailor-made for the extrovert. I was not an extrovert, but I made a pretty good show at playing one.

Entering full-time ministry at the age of eighteen was an adventure, but because of my family background, I generally knew what to expect. Life was going to be fairly predictable, I thought. I would begin by making it through college. I'd then become a pastor of a succession of churches, each one being somewhat larger than the

---

29   1 Corinthians 13:11 (NIV)
30   Proverbs 22:15 (KJV)

previous, because my denomination had a way of promoting the pastors while the churches stayed much the same. I would then be given a number of staff positions in various parts of the world before retiring gracefully – loved and appreciated by all (or most). Such confident predestination was my first mistake because what was about to happen could not have been predicted by anyone.

During the first few weeks of College a call went out for anyone with a guitar to assemble in a certain area, instrument in hand. Maybe they were having a purge of these 'worldly' instruments, I thought. Maybe a bonfire! Not fair! I had only hung my guitar on the wall next to a bullfight poster. It was not as if I actually played the decadent thing. I couldn't have if I had tried. It only had three strings, and I had not mastered any of them.

Out in the quadrangle I was relieved to find that they were not confiscating our guitars but rather making a big deal of them. We were to be photographed for the national and international press.

We learned later that a man called Frederick Coutts had just been elected the General of The Salvation Army and during his first press conference, he had mentioned something about his Army going out to the young people of the Sixties generation. "If they will not come to us, we'll go to them". That sort of thing. "And if they will not listen to our traditional brass bands and choirs, then we will go to them with our…" and then, from somewhere deep in his imagination, he said: "…guitars".

This all made for good copy. Visions of battalions of guitar twanging evangelists storming the bars, dance halls and clubs of Britain's major cities! General Coutts had an agile mind and a friendly disposition and I am sure he – and all the P.R. boys from Headquarters – thought a successful press conference was at an end, until some bright spark at the back asked "Where can we find these guitar playing Christians?" Good question!

Someone gave the press corps the idea that several guitars had, in fact, been seen lurking in the vicinity of our college. What they might not have known was that these probably belonged to female Scandinavian students who, back in the clean mountain air of their homelands, had belonged to large 'string bands', which accompanied the hymn singing at the local *Frelsesarmeen*. [31] The results, however, were closer to the Julie Andrews version of 'Edelweiss' than 'I Wanna Hold Your Hand'.

Nevertheless, the reporters and photographers clambered over to our college where, in response to the call for guitar owners, we were assembling outside our dorm houses, ready for our reprimand for being caught in possession of contraband musical instruments.

The cameras clicked away. We smiled, on cue, and duly appeared in national newspapers and magazines. Great fun! We would have bought copies had we had enough money. The most we could hope for was that our parents had seen our few minutes of fame.

To be fair, one or two students had made some attempts at contemporary music just a few weeks before. I recall hearing several students on a college stairway berating Peter Dalziel – who not only owned a guitar but had the temerity to actually play the thing. He had participated in an evening of 'Trad Jazz' at a local church. "But what if people get up and dance?" I heard an angry student yell, obviously confident that he was exposing the insidious sin-ridden root of such goings on in the House of God!

The trail of photographers continued for a few days until it was judged to be something of an interruption in our preparation for ministry. "We'll soon have an army of strummers" said one faculty member. "No preachers – just strummers." Someone stepped in to suggest that instead of all the guitar owners being photographed,

31   'Salvation Army' in Norwegian

they should choose a small group of students who possessed all the necessary qualifications. These were to know how to hold a guitar and to be capable of smiling nicely after the photographer counted to 'three'.

At that time of life, I could do both these things, simultaneously. In other words, I had a winning smile which I could accomplish on the fourth beat and I had recently worked out how to hold my guitar – in other words, *not* like a violin. Suitably qualified, I was chosen to be part of the 'Photo Group'. Our pictures appeared everywhere. National daily papers even ran comic strips about Salvationists playing on the street corner, but instead of their brass band instruments they had guitars, plugged into a nearby street light.

It was not long before this 'Photo Group' was asked to meet its greatest challenge yet. Namely, to actually play their instruments and "sing something"; and both at the same time! I believe it was the ingenuity of a Canadian Broadcasting reporter that started it all. He arrived without a camera, but equipped with a sound re-cording machine. "I want to hear you play, Ay!" He said. It didn't take me long to beat a hasty retreat from the scene. True, I had my guitar in place. I had even bought a full set of strings so that it didn't look quite so silly in the photographs. I'd even arranged the strings in the right order – the thick one first and the others in descending order of thickness. I could even play tunes on the top string, but chords were as yet a mystery to me.

That was it. I had enjoyed my time in the spotlight, with several newspaper photos to show my grandkids, with wistful whispers of "Those were the days". But as I walked away from the scene I was quickly stopped by Peter Dalziel. (Yes, the one who had suffered the slings and arrows on the stairway). "Don't leave me here!" He said, adding something about the fact that the rest of the group members were all girls. "But I can't play," I insisted.

Not to be outdone (or left with all those girls) Peter quickly taught me the chords of G..C.. and D seventh. "That's all we'll need" said Peter, aptly summing up the Sixties in a one-line prophecy. Having successfully completed my two-minute training session, we returned to the journalist who was patiently waiting on the other side of a shrub. Once he had switched on his recording device, we played "Everybody Ought to Know Who Jesus Is". It was easy for the first two lines. They were all in the G chord. But there was a conspicuous pause as I changed to the D7 for the third line. As for the chorus, that demanded a transition to the C chord, and we were through our first performance.

The days that followed proved to be the most hectic and dramatic of my young life. On the heals of the CBC recording – Moses-like by the bush in the college quadrangle - there came an invitation to play on a busy street corner and be filmed for BBC TV. A massive audience response to that broadcast resulted in us being invited for a second appearance. But this time it was in the famous BBC Broadcasting House and the "Tonight" program; Britain's major nightly news magazine show. The whole nation was watching!

I remember one moment of that night. It was the last time I allowed myself to be nervous. Because of my experience (all of several days) and my questionable ability to play actual melodies on my top string, I was appointed "Lead Guitar". That office gave me the responsibility of playing an introduction to our songs. After a couple of verses (or the same verse sung twice to "stretch it out a bit") I would then play a solo, and so on until we finished each epic attempt at Christian Pop Music.

So there I stood, along with the other group members, in the BBC studios. Someone said "Thirty seconds, studio" in that upper middle class accent that graced everyone in the BBC in that pre-Beatles era. After another twenty seconds or so the voice looked at me and, complete with hand gestures, he counted down "5 – 4 – 3…..". Then only his fingers did the talking…. "2 – 1", and he pointed in my direction.

That – I assumed – was my cue to begin our first song on live BBC-TV. Everything was live in those days. No second takes. No do-overs. No "Whoops, sorry… let's try that again". In the process of the last two seconds of his countdown I made a life changing decision. I just *had* to get it right. The whole country was watching. There were no alternative cable stations, no DVDs or videos to watch. It was black and white BBC-TV and the nation was staring at my hands. Get it wrong now, boy, and you'll live with it for the rest of your life!

You have heard the term "overnight success" but I wonder if you've ever met one. There was no other way to describe our as yet nameless little ensemble. On one of our TV appearances, we were viewed by an EMI producer who worked at the soon to be immortalized Abbey Road studios in London's St. John's Wood district. He invited us to make a 'test recording' although he might just as well have invited us to make a test flight, for all we knew.

We duly arrived in the studio and immediately stood around a microphone. By now we were quite professional and could actually identity a mic from the rest of the studio clutter. A producer walked in and noted that we had not taken the obligatory minutes (or sometimes hours) that other groups of the day took to get ready. We didn't know any better. We just knew how to start after someone pointed at us!

Eventually, he walked back into the control booth – a strangely bemused look on his face – and instructed an engineer (or was it one of the cleaners) to switch on the recording machine. And that's about all they did, other than add a ton of "echo" which, as Phil Spector later discovered, covered a multitude of sins. (But for Phil, maybe not quite enough!)

Our sound was appalling – at least to our ears now. But in those days it was the first attempt at Contemporary Christian Music which, up until then, had consisted of singing old hymns slightly faster while tapping one's foot.

Several songs were recorded and two were lifted out to be put on a single. "It's An Open Secret" and "Set The World A-Singing", both by Joy Webb, the faculty member of our college who had been given charge of our little group.

A short while after this adventure we were asked to sing on a Radio Luxembourg show, recorded at EMI House in London's Manchester Square. In those days, there was no commercial radio and very little rock music found its way onto the stuffy airways of "Auntie Beeb", the BBC. Then, back in the 1950s someone had come up with a solution. They taped shows in the UK, sent them out to the tiny independent nation of Luxembourg, then beamed them all over Europe, mostly for the enjoyment of the British and American soldiers posted throughout the Post War territories. In England, we would sit around the radio, listening for the strains of American Rock and Roll above the constant static that made it sound as if the singers were truly 'overseas'.

After the gig, a young lady came to me with a copy of Record Weekly in her hand. "What does it feel like to be in the Charts?" she said, smiling. I thought it was the lead in to a show business joke, and I felt too embarrassed to admit that I didn't know any show business jokes yet. All I knew were "Knock, knock" jokes and this didn't sound like one. I simply answered "Who's in the Charts?" "Well, *you are!*" was her reply. She opened up the paper and there we were, at number 28, one place above a little song called "She Loves You" by some other lads from my home town. I should hasten to add that "She Loves You" had been at No 1 for about six weeks and was on its way down after incredible success. But at least we met The Beatles as we made our way up.

Overnight – or at least over several short nights – we had found success – dramatically, abruptly and astonishingly. For several years after that, life was a whirlwind of international touring and packed concert halls in the capitals of Europe and Scandinavia. Abbey Road became the biggest and the most expensive toy I ever got to play with. We had our own weekly national TV slot on three networks. We were invited to Buckingham Palace for an audience with Her Majesty. On Christmas Day of 1967 we pre-recorded a morning TV program from a Manchester hospital, made a guest appearance on the Tom Jones Christmas Spectacular at lunch time, sang on BBC Songs of Praise in the evening and did our own "Song Break" show on ABC-TV half an hour later. All programs were taped days earlier and broadcast nationally. At the home of my then fiancé, Jean, it was an all-day listening and viewing marathon. We had just enough time to squeeze in Christmas dinner and The Queen's Speech!

Our little group was called The Joystrings. It was a name given to us by an EMI producer. We didn't like it at first, but it did us no harm. I admit that I enjoyed every minute of it. I was living what most kids could only dream of. But something else was taking place. Steadily, I was becoming disenchanted. Pride crept in. No, who am I kidding? It didn't creep in, it strode through the front door, unhindered. As our group became a competent and successful concert band, I easily forgot the God who had taken our childish early attempts and had used them to His glory.

When I stood before TV cameras or answered questions in a press conference, or especially when I appeared before vast crowds I knew better than to actually *show* pride. I was brought up better than that. But I allowed all the trappings of my world to feed something inside of me; something to do with my identity, security and self-image. Something only God's Holy Spirit could completely satisfy.

I was becoming an empty can of words.

I can truly say that I have been where others would only dream of going. In Abbey Road, I became acquainted with young men who were literally changing the cultural climate of the entire world, and not always for the better. I have sat for hours signing my name over and over again. I have waved from an open top car as it passed the crowds of the inner city of London and made laps around the Crystal Palace stadium, to the cheers on the on-looking crowds. I have been allowed into the recording sessions of one of the top three bands in the world as they taped their next single; a hallowed and secret place indeed! I have sensed the electric power of a great ballad capturing the hearts of a massive audience. I have traveled the nations, walked with celebrities and mingled with monarchs. I have stood alone on stage, armed only with an acoustic guitar, in front of 36,000 people. I have, in other words, climbed the heights from which many people think comes our identity and worth, but I finished that climb only to find that it can be empty up there.

My true identity was revealed to me some years later. The Joystrings had been prematurely closed down. In the last year of existence our ministry was as productive and fruitful as it ever had been. Concert halls throughout Europe and Scandinavia were packed whenever we came to town. Not least of all we had become a good band and most of all, hundreds, thousands were coming to Christ. We had been enjoying a long run with our weekly national series of programs called 'Song Break'. It was a great concept. We would set up stage in a large factory or business somewhere in England and after two days of camera rehearsals we'd put on a half hour program for the workers and their families. The result would be aired that Sunday evening for the whole nation to view. It was a great example of taking the relevance of the gospel to where the people really lived.

We were also due to make our first visit to the United States during the summer of 1968. This, however, was canceled after the organizers saw newsreels of the group singing in the London Playboy club. I learned years later how much more conservative America is to Europe! To us, it seemed yet another opportunity of taking our faith where it would have the most effect. To the Salvation Army in the States, it was reason enough to sever their ties with those radicals back in Swinging London! Even Billy Graham joined the fray by making known his disappointment that the Army had lowered its standards and gone to the world's ways with its contemporary music! I smile now, watching the very best of contemporary Christian music being used on Dr. Graham's crusades. We all grow and develop in our ministry – even that lovely man of God.

Some years later, when watching a History Channel retrospective of the U.S. in 1968, I recalled some of our songs – especially the folk-protest style that I was developing, which dealt with the issues of the day. I tried to picture what our reception might have been had we been asked to sing in segregated audiences in the Deep South, in the same year when young Christian protestors were being murdered in Alabama and Senator Bobby Kennedy and the Rev. Martin Luther King were assassinated. "We wouldn't have made it out alive" I conceded.

After the group's demise, I was invited to Headquarters to speak to the director of The Salvation Army's Public Relations Department. We enjoyed weekly interviews for several months. I wondered what it was all about as I made my way up to Headquarters from our little church in South London – which was arguably small enough to convince my peers that I wasn't getting any preferential treatment after the years of notoriety. Mostly, we spoke of what the "next step" could be, after The Joystrings. I argued against the group's closure and requested some opportunity for us to continue. He felt this would be unwise. It would look, he assumed, like we were dragging something along that should be allowed to die with the decade. To be fair to him, no-one then could have imagined that the music of that extraordinary decade would last well into the next century and that Sixties groups would be singing hits well into their own 'sixties' and beyond!

Then, at a pace seldom seen in Army history, the P.R. director was promoted, then promoted again, until he assumed the second highest position the Army could offer. A few years later he went on to the top position also. At this point, I suggested that maybe I should quit my regular interviews, so he arranged for me to meet with the man responsible for the Salvation Army's work in the UK. At least I was back under the auspices of my own territory - back in line with protocol.

It wasn't long before this man – a very loving and gentle leader who indulged me like a benevolent uncle – asked me "If you were to start a new group, who would you want to see involved? Bring me a list of names by the next time we meet." That was easy. I wrote out the names of those I knew would do the best job. My list began with 'Joy Webb and continued with Wycliffe Noble, Peter and Sylvia Dalziel and yes, Bill Davidson'. "But that's The Joystrings" he said. "We can't do that. We can't afford to use officer personnel for a project like this." We were aware that our leaders had faced a lot of criticism for allowing full-time ordained ministry personnel on such 'frivolous' duty! "You'll have to choose other people," he said.

So I made up a list of people I knew, and one or two I had heard of, and we created the follow-on band to The Joystrings. They were great young people, talented and happy to be involved. We certainly had a great opportunity handed to us, but one thing was out of place – if not two. First of all, whereas The Joystrings had been created out of nothing by the Hand of God, the next group was created out of something by the hand of man. Secondly, I was becoming a cynical, disillusioned and uncaring wreck. This was not a good combination for anyone's future.

Touring began again. The concerts lined up. We did some recording and a little TV. We made a few international trips, one of which was to The Netherlands. I have always enjoyed Holland. It is such a walking contradiction of itself. It is one of the most conservative and quaint of countries, and yet at the same time its spirit of permissiveness allows the most outrageous lifestyles to be tolerated.

Significantly, it was in the capital of 'de Nederlands' that I came to a spiritual climax. I had just finished a concert in Amsterdam. I left the hotel where I was staying and walked the streets, ending up in the Dam Square. I sat down on the cobbled street in the midst of hundreds of Hippies. Amsterdam was the European staging area for the Hippy Trail to the Ashrams of India, a road taken by many who would end up riddled with drugs and dying in some filthy hovel in Kabul, Afghanistan. For them, it was the road to oblivion.

I sat there thinking "These are my people - my generation. I should have something to give them. Some words to save them." Only a few hours before, on stage at one of our concerts, I had been challenging young people to surrender their lives to Jesus. Dozens had responded. But now, I sat out in the real world, empty in spirit, soul and body. I had become the epitome of what Jesus described when He judged the Pharisees for demanding burdens of others that they were not caring enough to carry themselves. [32]

A dirty bottle was handed to me. "Wat is het?" I inquired. "Melk v'n-kaas", came the blurred reply. My neighbor saw my confusion. "Cheese milk" he said, in perfect English — typically Dutch! I took it and let a sip pass my lips. Cheese milk it was. The most nutrition I had enjoyed in days. I had been sustained throughout that tour by some "sugar" supplied to me by one of the organizers. For some weeks, I had no stomach for real food.

"This is like communion" I thought, as I passed the bottle onto the next person, seated cross legged next to me. At that moment, something happened inside of me. The Holy Spirit was revealing that I was indeed communing with 'my people'. Like them, I also was lost, empty, lonely, and adrift. I held a deep resentment inside of me — many, in fact. Those were the days when my silliest

32   Luke 11:46

statement was seriously received as some deep, new philosophy (remember, this was the early 70s). I had enough talent and personality to fool most of the people for most of the time but God was not fooled, nor would His love allow me to remain in deception. Deep down, I had never completely fooled myself.

In the process of being recognized and accepted by millions I had lost my identity. In the wake of having my name known by the masses I had forgotten who I really was.

After being in ministry for more than a decade I was able to look inside at my sin scarred life; my self-praising soul; my desperate need for applause, recognition, affirmation; and what I saw revolted me. I longed for the simple child-like love I had once known for my Savior Jesus. I needed to lose myself, not in the destructive collective suicide of my generation, but in the tender self-giving love I had once known.

I now know that I have only one identity. It is not to be consumed by 'who I am' but rather to see who I am not. Without Jesus I am nothing. The Bible says that Jesus is the One who was "before all things, and in him all things hold together."[33] Without Him, then, is it any wonder that we fall apart?

Jesus said to his disciples, "If anyone would come after me, he must deny himself and take up his cross and follow me. For whoever wants to save his life will lose it, but whoever loses his life for me will find it. What good will it be for a man if he gains the whole world, yet forfeits his soul? Or what can a man give in exchange for his soul?" [34]

In the Royal Albert Hall in 2004 The Joystrings were invited back for a reunion of sorts. 'Forty Years On' and all that. I had imagined that we would play a concert. Like so many of our contemporaries we were all still active and could have easily played and sung

---

33   Colossians 1:17 NIV
34   Matthew 16: 24-26 NIV

as well, if not better, than in earlier days. But that was not to be. The unimaginative organizers of the event had us do a "walk on" to sing a couple of our softer songs, which had been long since adapted as traditional choruses within the denomination. We could so easily have packed a concert hall, even forty years on, and produced a lively, God-glorifying and even historic evening of thanksgiving and praise. Instead, they supplied a couple of young people, one on a grand piano and the other tapping lightly on a drum-set, to accompany the old folk! Had they supplied us with wheel chairs or Zimmer walker frames the picture would have been complete. I did, however, manage to say one thing I had long wanted to express. I quoted the following:

> Brothers, think of what you were when you were called.
> Not many of you were wise by human standards; not many were influential;
> not many were of noble birth.
> But God chose the foolish things of the world to shame the wise;
> God chose the weak things of the world to shame the strong.
> He chose the lowly things of this world and the despised things
> and the things that are not — to nullify the things that are,
> so that no one may boast before him. [35]

"That's what we should have been called" I quipped. "The 'Are-nots'. When The Joystrings began, we were not. No-one was. There was no such thing as Contemporary Christian Music. No-one could tell us what to do or how to do it. Our attempts were pathetic, but God used it anyway."

".... Those that *are not*, to confound the things that are."

Over those forty years I had discovered that my identity was defined not by who I was, am, or could be, but by who He is, always has been, and ever shall be... Amen.

---

35   1 Corinthians 1:26-29 NIV

5

Ears Pierced

I have decided that my political position is best described as 'Independent'. Even though I am an American pastor, an Evangelical, and a Charismatic to boot, and I have most often voted for the candidate to the Right of the spectrum, I have never been, shall we say, Conservative. In fact, I suppose I would credit myself with always tending to find the alternative idea when the crowd is gathering around a fixed position. Perhaps it's just a streak of rebellion in my Celtic soul.

Now and then, however, when confronted with certain issues of life, I surprise myself at how traditional I am – deep down. Such was the case, some years ago, when my wife and daughter expressed their desire to have their ears pierced. The very fact that they declared this on the same day they were walking with me in the Mall should have told me that this was not a new idea and was, in fact, the outward expression of a deeper and more devious plot which had been hatched long before it came to the surface.

I reacted more like a Victorian Salvationist than the cool guy I thought myself to be. Their pace slowed when passing each shop that blatantly betrayed its agreement with the females in my family with signs such as "Ears Pierced While You Wait" – as if there was an alternative of leaving them on lay-away and picking them up later!

Where did this conservative reaction come from? Of course the inevitable took place and both Kellie and Jean endured the pain and suffering for the joy that lay before them, and they have walked proudly with a variety of adornments dangling from their long-suffering ears ever since. In time Jean decided that her lobes were becoming too extended by the weight of the baubles; visions of African ladies with pegs the size of small coffee tables hanging from their ears rushed through my mind, and I was glad this epic era was over, for her at least. But Kellie continues on bravely to this day, dangling everything but the kitchen sink from her pretty ears. She is a school principal, so I can only guess that certain students are at least glad that they can hear her coming!

Then dawned a day which I simply didn't see coming. No word of knowledge or prophetic impulse gave me even the slightest warning. On that day, my son - all six feet and two hundred and twenty pounds of him – arrived home, complete with two ear-rings in each ear! That makes four in all! This was too much to take. "In my day, a man who wore ear rings was….." You can imagine the rest of my thought pattern. Granted, his ear ring era didn't last for ever and his image as a head-shaven ear-studded biker-WWF-wrestler gave way to the athletic but tender husband and Chihuahua-owning ministry man he is today.

In the midst of this I had to find some position. So, to show my love to him, or possibly to justify things and bring some inner peace to myself, I found a biblical precedent. Back in the Old Testament it states: "But if the servant declares, 'I love my master and my wife and children and do not want to go free,' then his master must take him before the judges. He shall take him to the door or the doorpost and pierce his ear with an awl. Then he will be his servant for life. [36]

Sounds pretty brutal, doesn't it? A little more crude than the 'Piercing Pagoda' in the local Mall! The ancient Hebrew version had the master taking his willing servant to the doorpost of his house and piercing his ear right there on the beam. The symbols of that act are profound.

- By being impaled to the door post the servant was, both practically and symbolically, tied into that household.
- The servant was no longer a slave by capture or purchase. He was there by his own commitment – even his love.
- No Hebrew was ever enslaved for life. His period of slavery would have been pre-designated by law. [37]
- But his meeting with and attachment to the doorpost of His master's home signified that he would henceforth be attached to and "give ear" to the business of his master, for the rest of his life.

It is interesting that all this was ratified "before the judges". [38] The Hebrew term used here is *elohhiym*. [39] This word usually speaks of Almighty God, but it can be used also to describe the justices or judges of the people. This deal was indeed ratified before them, but it was also confirmed before God Himself.

If there is one defining mark of a man of God, I believe it is that his ear is pierced. He is a willing servant.

Servanthood is an attractive prospect when preached right. Most of us would say a hearty 'Amen' to the idea. It's one of those

---

36   Exodus 21:5-6 NIV
37   Exodus 21:2
38   Exodus 21:6
39   Strong's word No. 433

universally accepted concepts. Few, however, walk it out along the way.

In the early 1970s, we left our Salvation Army roots. But for a year or so before our departure from our denomination we had experienced an amazing level of spiritual renewal. Genuine revival had spread from our little Salvation Army church across the town of Newark in the middle of England.

Our church was situated in a dilapidated hall which had once housed a silent movie theater. It stood at the cross-roads of England. Literally! Two historic roads had been laid by the Roman Empire sometime after Julius Caesar had made a brief visit to a couple of beaches in Kent. After a quick dip in the cold waters of The Channel he quoted to a nearby scribe: "Veni, vidi, vici" [40] He could probably have added: "and I caught a cold" because he immediately returned to the sunny climes of Italy and left his boys behind to do the road works. Britons have been digging up roads ever since.

From Exeter in the south west of the country the lads from Italy laid a highway called The Fosse Way all the way to Lincoln, well on the way to the northwest. Not satisfied, they followed this by laying The Great North Road which ran from Londinium [41] due north to the wilds inhabited by my forebears, the Celts, Picts, Britons and Scots. These ancient roads dissect at Beaumond Cross in Newark, Nottinghamshire [42] and at that cross roads stood our church.

I knew in my heart that it was 'make or break' for me in Newark. The empty husk of what was left of my better self was desperate to be filled. I devoured the New Testament which seemed more

---

40   'Veni, vidi, vici' - "I came, I saw, I conquered" – Julius Caesar 47BC
41   Londinium – later Anglicized as London
42   Beaumond Cross, Newark, England: stands at the junction of five streets or roads, and the place has been known as The Beaumond, or Le Beaumond, from time immemorial, being so named in a deed as early as 1310 AD, a thousand years after the Romans left the country.

alive to me than ever before. I came to the Acts of the Apostles and that's where the trouble started – around chapter two. "That's it", I reasoned. "I want nothing less than this." I was determined to find for myself all the power, peace and blessing so enjoyed by those New Testament Christians. I placed large posters outside our hall, past which thousands of people passed every day. One read: "Beware – This Building Catches Fire Next Sunday!" That Sunday, it did!

For years the faithful members of the local Baptist church had been praying for revival. Their building sat diagonally across Beaumond Cross from ours. They were stunned to find their prayers answered, but across the way, in The Salvation Army Hall, of all places!

Our traditional Salvation Army center began to sound and live like a contemporary expression of the New Testament Church during the days of the first Apostles. Most of the membership experienced a powerful encounter with the Holy Spirit, starting with the pastor and his wife. We started asking ourselves questions like: "If Pentecost was yesterday, what would the Church be like today?" And, "If The Salvation Army had just begun last week, what would our part of it look like and live like today?" Even: "If Paul the Apostle came into our meetings would he even recognize it as 'the Church'"?

We started praying for the sick. Not that we had never done so before. Salvationists care deeply for every aspect of life, spirit, soul and body, but we had to admit that we had never prayed publicly for sick people, laying hands on them, as the Scripture commands us, and expecting them to be healed.

The first time I suggested this in public an elderly man walked forward. His name was Bill. We called him Uncle Bill because of his seniority to the pastor! Out he walked and declared to everyone that he wanted to receive sight in his right eye, which was completely blind. Oh no, I thought. Why couldn't someone come out in the second day of forty-eight hour flu? Then at least we'd see some improvement, even if the praying didn't work. Nevertheless, we prayed and laid hands on Uncle Bill. He put his hand firmly over his good eye and opened the sightless one, wide, as if expecting to see something! After a few moments, I waved my hand in front of his blind eye. "No!" He shouted! "Not just partial healing. Not just partial sight!" "Partial sight"! I thought. I was amazed. I wasn't expecting anything. I think I was half expecting the other eye to go blind!

Our Salvationist practice was to not participate in the acts of Communion or Water Baptism. These things, we were taught, were an outward sign of an inner working of grace, and Salvationists were not concerned with the outward; an ironic position for a movement known for its flags, badges, marches and uniforms. So when it came to baptism we did not partake. But somehow that just didn't square with our heart to live as a New Testament Church, so we took more notice of the addendum to our Salvation Army doctrines, which allowed any Salvationist who desired to participate in Communion or Water Baptism to take themselves off to any local church that would have them and join in there. After which, of course, they would trot right back to The Army for the remainder of the Sunday.

In the Newark S.A. Church, everyone wanted to be baptized, with the exception of two or three who saw such a suggestion as the work of the Devil, or so their facial expressions implied. So, one Sunday evening I announced that anyone wishing to be water baptized could join Jean and me as we walked across the road to the Baptist Church where the pastor had agreed to baptize us. About seventy people joined the procession.

The next week I visited a local shop and bought a goblet which, we thought, would do just fine for serving Communion. And the Spirit of God visited us wonderfully as we "rightly discerned the Body of Christ". [43]

43   1 Corinthians 11:29

Dozens found Christ during those months, and we tried to keep up with the numbers by entering them in our 'Seekers Register', a book which had only a few entries marking the years before this outpouring. The day came when we drew a diagonal line across a page and wrote an apology to future keepers of the book because we were unable to keep up with what God was doing! We became like spiritual midwives, sometimes called out in the early hours of the morning, only to drive several miles to a house to burst through the door just to witness God doing some amazing things in the lives of the people. We didn't even need to be there. We just wanted to witness it all and enjoy what we called "The Splash-over".

It wasn't long before we were called down to the National Headquarters of our denomination. I had expected the call, and I did not fear it. The men and women who led our organization were all known to me. They acted more like loving uncles and aunts than 'leaders'. Seated in a committee room were the British Commissioner, The Field Secretary, whose job it was to appoint Army ministers to their positions, his two assistants, one or two other national officials. Quite a gathering, I thought.

To this day, I remember their kindness and concern for Jean and me. What we were experiencing had possibly not been seen in The Army during their lifetime, even if in the generation before it had been commonplace.

Sadly, however, no-one asked the questions I had expected. No-one inquired why or how so many people had been saved and in so short a period of time.

No-one questioned how or why our church members had exceeded their annual fund raising target by each deciding to give an entire week's salary to the Army's work, rather than to go door to door to the general public for the annual appeal.

No one asked how blind eyes had seen, how a witch had been redeemed and demons had fled the power of our meetings, or how dozens of Salvationists had a passionate love for Jesus that had never been there before.

No one queried how people had turned up to one of our unannounced weeknight meetings from the far north east of England and the far south west on the same night, saying: "We believe God told us to come here tonight."

No-one wondered why our teens and young married couples had stopped watching television, choosing rather to sit with their pastors each night to talk about, sing about and laugh about, Jesus.

No one questioned why or how the presence of God regularly entered our times of ministry to lay people out under His power; something which had happened regularly in the earliest days of the Army's history.

Rather, it was noted that I had been seen in town with a shirt which was more a red-ish grey than white – the regulation color. It was further noted that I used white paper for my correspondence instead of the color designated for local pastors, furthermore (and here we came the closest we got to a doctrinal statement) I was asked why I had used 'Army funds' to purchase a Communion Cup. I remarked that this was a great deal cheaper than buying even the smallest of our brass band instruments, but that didn't seem to impress my audience.

Let me hasten to add that we were not drummed out of the Army for these indiscretions. In fact, during that meeting I was offered "Whatever I wanted to do, wherever I wanted it to do it," so I asked to remain on in the Newark church for at least ten years. But it was stated that this would be "detrimental to my career".

I admit that in the past I had been known to be something of a rebel. Years before going to Newark, I had given up wearing the Salvation Army cap. It looked downright silly on top of my thick shoulder length hair. Or rather, I looked silly, not the cap. During my first stint of duty on the Army's National Headquarters there even came a day when the General of The Salvation Army sent a memo to the national leader of the British Territory. (At the time, these two men occupied offices just a few doors down the corridor from each other). The memo read: "Captain Davidson, seen in St. Paul's Precinct, without cap." The leader of the British Territory told me later of his reply: "If the General has time to write a memo to The British Commissioner about Captain Davidson's cap, he is in a different army than I."

That really appealed to my rebellious side - or was it a prophetic side? Perhaps in several areas of life we were simply thirty years ahead of our time? Some of what we lived out as a revolutionary form of Salvationism is now embraced within the ranks, for better and for worse!

The Newark episode brought me to a different state of mind. This was no reaction of a rebel. My own encounter with the Holy Spirit had come after a year or so of seeking and praying. I was desperate. After years of acclaim and attention, I was empty and longing to be filled – and God did not disappoint.

Jean and I both recognized that although we thanked God for the solid foundation our Army years had given us, our ear had been pinned to a different doorpost. Not the doorpost of another movement, denomination or organization, but to the doorpost of God's Household.

Some interpreted our departure by assuming we thought that remaining in the Army held us back, in some way. Others concocted stories of such a nature that would have justified our dismissal. The fact is we simply felt we had no right to expect the 'Dear Old Army' to accommodate the changes we not only sought but had already experienced. So, although leaving the ranks was an unthinkable prospect for a couple of 'Army kids' like Jean and me, we took solace from the fact that the path we now chose was once trodden by The Army's founder, William Booth himself, when he left his denomination, The Wesleyan New Connection, to follow another path.

We joined up with Youth With a Mission. We found little difficulty in taking the step away from our denomination. We realized that the Army cared for its pastors from Bible College to grave, but we happily accepted the loss of security in ministry and, in later life, the absence of a pension plan or retirement accommodation. Long before our time, The Army had devised a plan that, should an officer resign from his or her commission, they would forfeit all contributions to their pension. Unthinkable and unethical in most quarters, but legalized under The Army's Constitution.

We were young. Our daughter Kellie was five and Craig just three (our third child, John William, was to be adopted out of Colombia some years later). Thoughts of financial security and retirement were farthest from our minds. We were stepping out in faith, as obedient servants should.

Our departure was also cushioned by our new experiences in the greater Christian world beyond the ranks in which we had been raised, much of which, to our embarrassment, had no idea that The Salvation Army was even a church and not simply a philanthropic organization. Eventually, when we traveled extensively in The United States, we grew tired of explaining that we were brought up in The Salvation Army, after which we hastily added: "Which, in England, is an evangelical denomination" – much to the surprise of our listeners. And so we would begin a brief overview of The Army's spectacular history.

After those public years of acclaim and attention, I was delighted to take a back seat at last – the servant seat! The joke about my life is that I am a very private person. I am not an extrovert, but like many actors I can put on the show of an outgoing personality, when necessary. I am from North Scottish stock; the kind of folk that sing their hymns much slower and keep themselves to themselves. There is a Norse saying that goes: "Aye, aye," he said. "And he said no more that day!"

Soon after our marriage I realized how offensive it was for Jean to keep hearing me state: "Personally, I'd just like to be on my own on a desert island." Of course, I quickly learned to add, "With Jean!" So when life slowed down a lot, I was ready to take on the quieter servant role.

I enjoyed sitting in the YWAM School of Evangelism and soaking in the amazing teaching of men like Winkey Pratney, Gordon Olsen and Harry Conn. Even though I'd been exposed to a great deal more in ministry than all those around me, I was happy not being the leader. I could now be the servant. Wasn't that what God would desire for me?

Thoughts such as these were going through my mind when we received a visit from the one and only Barry McGuire, the giant of the Sixties whose "Eve of Destruction" had hit the charts in '65. Now the gentle giant was on fire for Jesus and due to visit our YWAM base in Crawley, in the county of Sussex, just around the corner from Gatwick Airport.

I helped a little with the organizing of the event and was content to sit in the wings during the concert. It was a pleasant change for me. I was happy at how my project of becoming more servant-like was coming along. I sat there, watching Barry sing with his acoustic guitar, break a few strings and keep the crowd pleasantly involved while he put the new strings in place. I wasn't jealous of the spot-light. In fact, I realized that I was now in such a servant attitude that I would happily carry Barry's guitar case for him, the rest of my life. I could picture it; Barry arriving at an event, crowds greeting him gleefully. Barry closely followed by a servant-like Anonymous Guitar Case Carrier.

Case closed (if only a guitar case). I had passed the test. I had a genuine servant-heart. However, it was at about that stage in my thoughts that the Holy Spirit stepped in, to show how utterly unimpressed He was with my 'filthy rags righteousness'. [44]

A conversation began in my mind. I imagined God saying:

> "So, you'd be happy to carry Barry's case?"
> No problem. I knelt before the Lord – eyes suitably lowered, showing my humility.
> "What about Harry McTavish?" God said.
> I asked who this McTavish character might be.
> "Oh, just someone I know," said God. "Would you be willing to carry *his* case?"
> I thought about it for a moment.
> "So, this McTavish guy, he's got something wrong with his arms that he couldn't carry his own case?"

Of course the lesson was dawning on me. There I sat, in the wings, so humble, so servant-like that I was ready to carry the famous guy's case, but forget the unknown Harry McT! When it came to servanthood, I needed a course in the real thing.

More than thirty years have passed since then, most of which I have spent in what the world would describe as relative obscurity. God led us to a small village in the Adirondack Mountains of Upstate New York. Ever since, I have been called to take up the office which has servanthood written all over it: the office of Church Planter. This job is remarkably different from the passage of a minister in a more traditional setting.

---

44   See Isaiah 64:6

Within our denomination, we could predict with unerring accuracy the steps and stages through which we would progress towards our pre-dated retirement. But as a church planter life is far less predictable.

As a junior pastor in a denominational setting I could expect to be given the responsibility of a small church. Jean and I cared for such congregations in Streatham and Brixton in London's south east communities. Not a great deal was expected of us. We would do well if we were able to initiate anything unusual in the life of the church, as we did in both these corps [45] when we added dozens of children to our role by opening exciting Kids' Clubs. Sooner or later we knew we would be posted elsewhere, and if again we did a reasonable job, the next posting would be to a larger church. Repeat that pattern several times and a minister might then be posted to a headquarters position, and he or she would be 'on their way'. In this way, the ministers were promoted, but their progress was not often matched at the local corps level. The congregations often remained the same or disappeared by attrition or atrophy.

I remember when this revelation first came to me. I was nineteen years young when I was posted, along with a team of students for which I was responsible, to a "Training Corps" in the City of Westminster. In this particular part of South West London, there are one or two significant Christian congregations. There is Westminster Cathedral, the headquarters of Catholicism in Britain. This was the place where, when I was mistaken for the international leader of The Salvation Army, I was invited to attend a major function and ended up enthroned by the high altar, along with other national and denominational leaders! But that's entirely another story, for another chapter. Then of course there's Westminster Abbey, where I and my fellow Joystrings were invited to help celebrate the church's 900th Anniversary! Across the road from the Abbey stands Westminster Central Hall, the heart of Methodism.

---

45   Salvation Army churches are given the military term 'corps'.

The church to which I was appointed was a very different matter. It was housed in a small hall with a coal stove at one end, around which in the winter months we would sit huddled against the cold.

When I first arrived I was welcomed by a number of middle aged ladies who seemed a little too eager in their greetings. At first I thought they were simply overjoyed to be shaking hands with the boy they saw on TV each week, but eventually I got the picture. They all remembered another William Davidson, who had come to that same church for training in the early years of his ministry. He was none other than my father! We were much the same build and height. The hair was the same color and my walk, mannerisms and even the set of my mouth reminded people of him. So no wonder these ladies were a little excited to speak to this living image of a young pastor who they all had liked so much when they, and he, were teenagers!

Do you see the sadness in this? Here I was, thirty years later, ministering at the same small church as my father had all those years before. By the time I appeared at this training corps my father was responsible for several dozen churches as an overseer. He had walked successfully along the path of promotion, but sadly the little church in Westminster had stayed the same. "Mutton bones", we used to call that kind of church in the denomination. In my adopted homeland we would call it "slim pickins". But the young denominational pastor need not be too concerned. If he did reasonably well, or, even if he didn't, he would be moved along the line soon enough, to something with a little more meat, a more 'successful' church: a promotion.

How different that career pattern is to that of a church planter, especially one outside the security of an established denomination. Each time he sets in the foundation of a new ministry, he has to personally start again, from scratch. He had better have a pretty good grasp of servanthood before attempting to take that path.

The church planter must of necessity be ready to do all the menial jobs, just like a junior minister, starting out. He must have the goods behind the pulpit and his pastoral skills must be acceptable, because when it comes to prospective members being attracted to his church, initially, he is all that they will see.

He must also have a degree in chair-putting-out, be a master of sweeping up after meetings and his doctorate had better include some courses in making sure the lights are out and the doors locked after the last person has left the building. He must accept that when his fledgling congregation says "Why don't they do this, or that", that he is the 'they' to whom they are referring. He must also have a high level of skill in living on next to nothing, and it would benefit him greatly if he were to have a wife who could shop for the essentials while having a modest estimate of what those essentials actually are. He and she must, above all, have servant hearts.

Servants are ready to work toward the purpose of their lives even if it means no-one takes any notice. Servants are happy to see the job done, even if someone else gets the attention and subsequent glory. Servants cannot be insecure or question their self-worth. They must be convinced that their lives have value and significance that come not from what they do, or in the acknowledgement and appreciation of others. Their value must come from the simple fact that they know 'Who' created them and that God never makes anything without it having a unique purpose of His own choosing and design. Living out that purpose, on a day-by-day basis, is all a servant needs in order to be totally fulfilled. That simply means doing whatever is needed, to see that purpose accomplished.

I cannot count the times and the ways that the attitude of servanthood has been tested in my life. I remember one season in particular.

In the mid 1990s Jean and I felt called to plant a church. It would be the fifth local church, among other ministries, planted out from our original American ministry, Church of The Nations, in Lake Luzerne, New York. At first we held meetings in a variety of places including cell meetings in private homes. The local Grange Hall saw our first public gatherings. A hundred years before, The Grange had been the place where farmers would have met to discuss their market prices in the days when Mr. Ingles had set up home in his "Little House on The Prairie". He was a member of the local 'Grange'. [46]

After that we occupied a number of sites. The lodge at a local ski area proved a picturesque and popular venue but our season of experimenting with Sunday evening meetings at a local Wesleyan Church didn't go down too well although we always remember the kindness of the local congregation. Lastly, before we built our present ministry center, we occupied a gymnasium which was used throughout the week by the local YMCA gymnastic club. It had a distinct odor of sweaty socks, so we arrived each Sunday morning to put out the chairs and set up the p.a. system armed with our guitars, drums, Bibles – and several cans of Lysol deodorant and disinfectant spray.

Eventually, we stepped out in faith and bought a piece of property. Just over three acres, complete with an old farm house and what was left of a barn. We invited the local fire department to burn down the barn. We spent countless hours – and dollars – to renovate the farm house, and then we broke ground in the area which would house our new ministry center.

Building projects are the bane of pastors' lives and the perfect test of his servant heart, but I knew exactly how I would set about this one. I would use a method tried and tested in Lake Luzerne, only fifteen miles away. We would have some professional come in and do the basic framing of our new building, and then I would gather a large crew of volunteers to finish off the project.

46   "Little House on The Prairie" A series of books by Laura Ingles Wilder.

In Luzerne we had only to mention that we needed to clear a forest and make a mile-long, sixty feet wide access road on the church property, and there would be a dozen chainsaws buzzing the next Saturday morning. Thirty people would be clearing brush, including teens and children, and a dozen or so more would be tending brush fires. Three Saturdays of work later the job was done and our road was open. It was the same when a house had to be built, a soccer field cleared or repairs made to the church property. If that's how we did it in Luzerne then that's how we'd do it in Queensbury. And that is where I made a major miscalculation.

Upon hearing of my plans, especially the part about the dozens of happy volunteers, the husband of one of our members said: "That's not how we do it in Queensbury. Over here we throw money at it."

What did he know!? He wasn't even saved at the time! Anyway, we didn't have any money to throw. This guy obviously didn't understand how God worked. At least that was my initial thought. In time I realized he had prophesied as accurately as any seasoned Spirit filled believer because when it came time for our *volunteers* to finish off the project there were but a handful of us. We had two or three men who actually knew what they were doing… one or two more willing hands…and me.

I was given the task of framing out the basement so my building partner and I set about the task of creating the rooms according to the architect's plans. There we were: me, my partner, and his dog; his *Seeing Eye* dog. Yes, my partner was blind. So when I took charge it truly was "The Blind Leading the Blind!" I must hasten to add that this man was a phenomenon. He was a cabinet maker and carpenter *extraordinaire*. He certainly made life interesting. For one thing, he removed all the safety guards from his table saw. "But if I leave them on" he said, "I wouldn't be able to feel the saw blade." It was pointless to try to convince him that this was why the guards were there in the first place!

As the months wore on we worked hard in that basement. Most days and several evenings each week you could find us, walking, kneeling or lying, on the cold concrete floor. And when I say 'cold', I mean that when it was minus15 degrees outside it was probably minus 20 on that concrete. Arthritic pain started into my hands and spread throughout my body. Every bone I owned ached and what little muscle I had groaned for relief. Wearing two or sometimes three sets of work clothes did little to ease the gnawing freezing cold that all but dragged me to a standstill. But something else was gnawing away at me as well.

'What am I playing at?' I would think, as I dragged by body home each night, covered in sawdust. I was well into my fifties and yet here I was, doing what a young twenty-something pastor should do if he were but starting out.

Then another thought came to mind. Several of my contemporaries in the old denomination had just been promoted to prestigious positions at the top of the denomination's leadership network. Their added responsibilities would bring with them an easier lifestyle, I reasoned. But that was not my lot in life. It seemed I had been a pioneer throughout my ministry - always taking the next hill - never allowed to 'settle'.

At that very time I heard the news that two close friends of mine, who were just a few years my senior, had been elected as the international leaders of the Salvation Army — one after the other. Whether or not I would have been elected to such lofty positions with the Army is debatable, but lying there in the cold, in my work clothes, I could not but help comparing my lot with theirs, and not favorably.

Our ministry center is now in place and the church has grown. I see and hear the crowds in Sunday Celebration roaring back their praise to one of the best worship bands I've ever heard. So it's laughable to think that I doubted that I should have served in the way we were called to in the earlier pioneer days of Church of The

King. [47] I would not think of trading my lot for any alternative, however much easier it might appear. I now enjoy a great set of friends around me. I am surrounded by a wonderful local church. For the last fifteen years I have met weekly with pastors of the great ministries in our area under the banner of Adirondack Churches Together. [48] We are committed to walking as friends, colleagues and partners in our ministries. We regularly visit our extended family ministries in Colombia, Wendy and Barbara, Eduardo and Esperanza, Luis and Clara. I meet regularly with the members of the coordinating teams of Alliance International Ministries. My 'Band of Brothers' in AIM include John Dean from Texas, Dan Haas from Illinois, John Guido from Ecuador, Terry King from Maryland, John Cairns from Australia, Luis Rodriguez from Colombia and Philipson Nagbe from Liberia. These are covenant brothers and our lives are open to each other. They and so many others stand in support of me and my family. I genuinely love preaching the Word of God to my home church and, as I've hinted, our worship times are powerful. Most of all, Jean and I enjoy three generations of our family sitting at Sunday lunch time. I live in a truly beautiful area of the world, and I regularly travel the globe for ministry and for pleasure.

What more could a man ask? But back in the pioneer days of this church I fell for the foolish trick of comparing my temporary lot as a 'carpenter and builder's mate' to those of my contemporaries back in the old denomination who, incidentally, are now retired and, as the song from 'White Christmas' says: "What do you do with a general when he's no longer a general?".

Pioneering a church is hard - very hard. It feels like starting over – again. It feels like demotion. It feels like servanthood!

The truth I learned during that season is that we should never graduate from the school of servanthood. I have worked with men who have somehow convinced themselves that they are above the

---

47   Church of The King – www.cotk.net
48   Adirondack Churches Together (ACT) - See "adkchurches.com"

menial tasks of life. I guess they've decided that their experience or their giftedness has elevated them above the role of the servant. To me, that seems so hollow.

In our churches we have a saying: "You never get promoted beyond putting out the chairs." That doesn't mean that we should all be doing the same things we did when we were young. Now I am a senior citizen, I am happy to have young leaders around me that tell me to step aside if something needs lifting – and I'm even happier to obey them and take my place as a spectator. I see in their honoring of me and my 'older' buddies, the testimony of a good upbringing in the things of God. But the heart attitude of servanthood should never disappear from a leader's arsenal, however senior he may become.

One of those friends who became the General of The Salvation Army once asked me "How do you see yourself in forty years?" I was eighteen at the time and he a lofty twenty six and a faculty member of my Bible College. I saw myself preaching in the Westminster Central Hall, a benevolent old leader of The Salvation Army.

How wrong I was! For a start, I now know that forty plus eighteen is not old! But I also see what a poor image I had of success in those boyhood days. I had little understanding of servanthood – of having my ear pierced and pinned to a kingdom vision.

I am reminded of my old school song: "Forty years on, when afar and asunder, Where will those be who are singing today? [49] Few boys envision themselves becoming servants; they plan to be leaders! But that is where the kingdom of God comes into focus and confounds the values of this world.

The kingdom truth is that leaders are servants and servants are leaders. The moment that exemplifies this is recorded in the gospels. It begins with a narrative that should have the 'Theme from

49   An adaptation of the Harrow School Song

Star Wars' played in the background. It certainly sounds as if something all-mighty is about to take place.

> Jesus, knowing that the Father had given all things into His hands, and that He had come from God and was going to God, rose from supper and laid aside His garments, [50]

Look at that first phrase: "knowing that the Father had given all things into His hands". That speaks of Christ's identity, absolute authority, unlimited power, and unquestioned ability. This verse states that Jesus knew who He was, where He had come from and where He was going. So now what was He about to do? The verses continue:

> (He) laid aside His garments, took a towel and girded Himself. After that, He poured water into a basin and began to wash the disciples' feet, and to wipe them with the towel with which He was girded. [51]

I have heard it preached that *despite* the fact that Jesus was God, He acted like a servant. I disagree. I believe it was not *despite*, but *because* Jesus was God, He acted like a servant. Until we catch that reality we will never see Servanthood as God sees it.

I realize that Paul stated 'Though he was God, he did not demand and cling to his rights as God. He made himself nothing; he took the humble position of a slave and appeared in human form,' [52] which invites the idea of *despite* the fact that He was God. But Paul's words at that moment are from man's perspective, to help us realize the cost of Christ's decision to appear in human form. But to do so, He did not change His character!

Servanthood is tested not only in 'ministry' endeavors, but every

---

50   John 13:3,4 NKJV
51   Verses 4-6
52   Philippians 2:6,7 NLT

day. Any married couple will testify to that. Those who fight for women's liberation (and why should they not when confronted with the arrogance and ignorance of so many Christian ministry men towards females?) might make much of the verse: "Wives, submit to your husbands as to the Lord." [53] But look what comes in the next paragraph: "Husbands, love your wives, just as Christ loved the church and gave himself up for her." [54] That means the man should be willing to surrender, yield up and entrust himself to the woman. An easier way of describing that lifestyle is caught in one word: "Servanthood".

If you ever feel inclined to become a servant follower, just make sure you are following a servant. Check his "ear". If he has truly met with God, it will be pierced.

---

53   Ephesians 5:22 NIV
54   Verses 25, 26

6

The Greatest and the Least Important

Servanthood deserves at least one more chapter. It's that important. In fact, it's everything. It supersedes gifting and ability. It is not only a priority in a leader's life, it's the one vital qualification for him to be a genuine leader.

How many gifted people have I met who have never learned how to be successful in God's eyes, in other words, how to be a servant? Let me count the ways!

Over the years Jean and I have led several ministries which have taken on the challenge of preparing young people for life and ministry. We have been directors in the Discipleship Training Schools of Youth With A Mission in the UK and Canada, and we've led our own Ministry Schools and The Service Corps in Church of The Nations and more recently, Service International, under our son Craig's directorship and out of Church of The King and our ministry family of Alliance International Ministries. [55]

---

55   Alliance International Ministries (AIM) See: www.aimteam.org

In the first few days of these schools we lead the students through a basic time of orientation and 'Servanthood' is an essential lecture topic.

On one occasion, we noticed a young man who seemed seriously distracted. This same young man was constantly interrupting the flow of life in the school, including the lectures, with demands which were geared not so much toward the common good, but toward his own preferences. He had no understanding of working within a team or a community. He was regularly the last to volunteer for duties – in fact, he seldom volunteered - the last to appear in class for lectures, the last to emerge from the dorm when his team was going somewhere. He was the last for…. Well, you get the picture. His attention span in class was minimal, and that's being generous.

About the third day of school the director had the boy in for an interview. We realized that not all students would be prepared to leave their everyday life and knuckle down to study. Many show how they have been overly catered to by an adoring parent, in whose eyes the child could do no wrong. One of our 'jokes' during orientation was to reveal to students that they had left their 'slave' at home, meaning their mother, who had picked up after them for the eighteen previous years! We also recognized that some students might even have legitimate problems such as an Attention Deficit Disorder, so we were anxious to discover this young man's particular challenge and do what we could to help. That, after all, was what the school was all about. But our ability to meet his special needs came to a grinding halt when we heard his response to the gentle coaxing of his director. "Oh, I know," he said. "But you see the problem is that I've heard all this before, and I am already a leader."

That statement, out of the mouth of any teenager, is worth a benevolent smile and a pat on the head. But when it comes from a young man as gifted as this particular boy, it makes my stomach turn. It is potentially toxic, not only to him and to those close to him in the years to come, but to the Body of Christ.

Leadership in Christian Ministry can be a wide open door for some who would otherwise be labeled as having narcissistic tendencies. Narcissistic Personality Disorder is a mental disorder in which people have an inflated sense of their own importance and a deep need for admiration. They believe that they're superior to others and have little regard for other people's feelings. But behind this mask of ultra-confidence lies a fragile self-esteem, vulnerable to the slightest criticism. [56] Working as a pastor, especially in certain Charismatic ministries where the leader's level of accountability can be chosen by the leader himself, it is all too possible for a person to begin to take his own giftedness as a testimony to God's affirmation.

But gifts are never a measure of a person's ability or value. They are gifts, given by the grace of God. In fact, the New Testament root word for *gift* and *grace* is the same thing.[57] When a person counts a gift as an attribute, he denies the grace.

The level of gullibility in those who follow such leaders is as dangerous as the leader's own challenges. Sadly, it is sometimes hard to discern who is more to blame; those who lead a crowd astray, or those who blindly follow, wagging their lack of discernment behind them.

A 'gifted leader' is so often seen as one who has a way with words, a winning smile; one who can easily attract and gather a following. He will soon be acclaimed as one who 'has the anointing'. In reality, it would be better for him were he to wash the dishes, vacuum the carpet and set out the chairs, at least for a season. His true gift will find room for him – in God's time and place – and in that meantime, some depth of character might be formed – for the common good.

56   Mayo Foundation for Medical Education and Research (MFMER).
57   Strong's words 5485 & 5486 *(charis & charisma)*

The biblical standard is clear. Leaders should be 'men worthy of respect, sincere, not indulging in much wine, and not pursuing dishonest gain. They must keep hold of the deep truths of the faith with a clear conscience. They must first be tested.' [58] Notice: leadership qualities have been demonstrated. They are then tested – not to see if leadership is there; that's already obvious. The test is to plumb the depth of character. '…and then if there is nothing against them,' Paul continues, 'let them serve as deacons.' So, even after the testing, they're ready for servanthood. The rest will follow.

We have all seen some wreckages in our time! Who, of my generation, can forget the awful experiences of viewing the televised and tearful confessions of those who had been idolized beyond accountability, simply because of their giftedness?

During our time with Youth With a Mission in Canada our YWAM base was visited by a Christian consultant. Such was his influence that he claimed to have the ability to "pick up the phone, and you'll be a cover story within weeks." And he was speaking to a multi gifted ministry. The YWAM base in Cambridge, Ontario, was packed with gifted and anointed people, including my friend Colin Harbinson whose dance-drama 'Toymaker & Son' still stands in my estimation as one of the dramatic highlights of our generation.

There were others who excelled in music, drama, dance, journalism, broadcasting – and then there was me with a couple of new solo albums under my belt, having just finished "Star Wars of Darkness & Light" – still my favorite album! [59]

The consultant first challenged us to seek God's will as to whether he should work for us. He then stated that he had a question to ask before going any further. "Who can say 'no' to you?" He

---

58   1 Timothy 3:8-10 NIV
59   'Star Wars of Darkness & Light' – Bill Davidson – Master's Collection (Canada) Grapevine Records (UK) GRV-119

asked. The group of leaders smiled as we began to consider that everyone else in the room had that prerogative in all the others' lives. Most of us were married, so we could add a few more significant others to the list.

We realized what he was getting at when he told of a similar reaction as ours when he had put the same question to YWAM's founder, Loren Cunningham. Loren laughed as he called his wife into the room. "Darlene, this man wants to know who in my life can say no to me." You can imagine whose name went first on the list!

The consultant stated that, unless a satisfactory answer could be given to that question he would not consider working with the ministry. In other words, he was only willing to work with servants, not 'masters'. He then went on to tell us the story of a world famous preacher who had asked for his help. The consultant's first question was presented to the preacher. The preacher had laughed as he turned to the man who was his executive director. "Hey, tell him who can say no to me." The other man turned to the consultant and said: "Sir, no-one says no to _____ _____!"

I wish I had been there to see the expression on their faces as the famous consultant abruptly left the room.

It was about two years later, as I sat late one night in a hotel room in Florida, watching that same preacher weeping his way through his public humiliation. No one had ever said no to him — including, it would seem, the Call Girls he frequented. If only he had learned to be a servant.

Service International, [60] is our training ministry designed for young people, many of whom are in their 'gap year' between one stage of their education and their next important step. The motto of SI is:

---

60   Service International: See: "serviceinternational.cotk.net"

"Service International – For The Greatest Among You."

That would be downright presumptuous were it not for the context of that phrase. It was Jesus who said "The greatest among you will be your servant." [61]

I once heard Bishop Wellington Boone ask a men's conference this question: "Who's in charge in your home? Who holds the authority?" He answered his own question. "Why, the woman of the house, of course! She holds the place together. She's the one people refer to for advice and direction. And why? because she serves more than the man. And servants lead!" As Bishop Wellington would say, "Don't shout me down, now!"

There is a great universal law. It is the Law of Love. It is a direct expression of God's character. All creation works by things giving themselves, sometimes even dying, in order to reproduce their kind and continue the cycle of life. That's what love is: a free-will gift of oneself to the object of one's affection.

I remember back in the 80s being introduced to the idea of the "39 One Anothers". I think we've found a few others since then, but the basic idea was to list all the times we are exhorted to do something for and to "one another". Exhorted to serve.

Have fellowship with one another	*1 John 1:7*
Love one another	*John 13:34,35*
Belong to one another	*Romans 12:5*
Be devoted to one another	*Romans 12:10*
Honor one another in showing love	*Romans 12:10*
Rejoice with one another	*Romans 12:15*
Weep with one another	*Romans 12:15*
Have the same mind for one another	*Romans 12:16*
Don't judge one another	*Romans 14:13*
Accept one another	*Romans 15:7*

---

61   Matthew 23:11 NIV

Counsel one another	Romans 15:14
Greet one another	Romans 16:16
Wait for one another	1 Corinthians 11:13
Care for one another	1 Corinthians 12:25
Serve one another	Galatians 5:13
Bear one another's burdens	Galatians 6:2
Be kind to one another	Ephesians 4:32
Forgive one another	Ephesians 4:32
Submit to one another	Ephesians 5:21
Bear with one another	Colossians 3:13
Encourage one another	1 Thessalonians 5:11
Build up one another	1 Thessalonians 5:11
Stir up one another	Hebrews 10:24
Be hospitable to one another	1 Peter 4:9
Minister gifts to one another	1 Peter 4:10
Be clothed in humility toward one another	1 Peter 5:5
Speak no evil of one another	James 4:11
Don't grumble against one another	James 5:9
Confess your faults to one another	James 5:16
Pray for one another	James 5:16

All of these are clothed in the context of some of the most challenging words ever written on papyrus and certainly no greater challenge exists in human behavior. Paul wrote: 'Do nothing out of selfish ambition or vain conceit, but in humility consider others better than yourselves.' (Selah: Pause! Breathe! Think!) Now Continue: 'Each of you should look not only to your own interests, but also to the interests of others.' There's more… 'Your attitude should be the same as that of Christ Jesus: Who, being in very nature God, did not consider equality with God something to be grasped, but made himself nothing, taking the very nature of a servant.' [62]

Imagine a church full of people living out those simple statements. It would be a church full of servants…. a church full of leaders. A church bearing the mark of God on its every member.

---

62   Philippians 2:2-7 NIV

7

Directionally Challenged

At some point in the future there will be a man steering his interplanetary transporter through deep space. Sitting beside him will be a woman saying "Would it kill you just to stop and ask directions"!

Men are directionally challenged because they feel they have a sixth sense about getting there without a map. They know better than Google, Map Quest or even their GPS (or "SatNav" as the British call it). Men believe the title "female navigator" is an oxymoron, whereas women just sigh because the driver is the moron. Men believe it is a sign of weakness – no doubt found in the fairer sex – to need such props as helpful natives or street signs. "Those State employees who put the signs up in the first place – what do they know!"

Jean has enjoyed a good laugh many a time when I have declared that we should be going "in that direction," at which time I wave my hand vaguely towards the windshield of the car. When asked how I know, I declare that "the moss is on the north side of the trees" or "Well, the sun is over, there and it's almost two o'clock."

This mythic wisdom which no doubt transcended through the generations from my Celtic forefathers works just fine if:

a. there actually *is* moss on the trees,
b. the sun is out
c. if we're not in New York City, where there are very few trees and what moss there is, is covered with graffiti!

Having met with God, a person for ever after has a destination, but the exact route to that destination is often a bit vague, at least, it looks like it to those observing from a distance. But we get there, by God's grace, even if in the process we might have lost our coordinates a few times along the way. And I'm not talking about our destination being Heaven, or The City of God. I refer to the various subsidiary destinations God gives us during our stay here on Planet Earth.

That sense of knowing where we're going is called 'vision'. It is the inner knowledge of a sense of overall purpose and destiny. It's exciting stuff. It's the motivational fire that ignites the days when we lose a little of life's natural heat. More often than not, vision is the beacon that leads us home when our mistakes, or the opposition of others, or the simple inertia of the majority could well have us losing our way or at least ending up on some siding.

In my younger years, I had seldom heard the term "visionary". Indeed, it wasn't until I entered Youth with a Mission that I even discovered the well known verse that exhorts us to 'make the vision plain'. [63] Then people began to claim that I was a visionary. It was not always meant as a compliment. Often the explanation began, "You see the trouble with visionaries is...."

---

63   Habakkuk 2:2,3 NKJV

I have a daughter who is a visionary. She fully expects The King's School [64] in little Lake Luzerne, N.Y. to flourish into an establishment known for its excellence and influence. It burns in her and out of her whenever she speaks about King's.

Our move to Lake Luzerne in the first place was a visionary step. To leave city life in the UK and Canada, with ministry opportunities popping up around us, to settle in a mountain village with a population around two thousand was not a reasonable thing to do.

I knew God had said "This is your place, these are your people, this is home to you." In answer to those who asked "But, why?" – and they were not a few – I would simply state that I believed that this village and this southern Adirondack area would one day become a global hub from which we would go out to the nations and, in return, see people from the nations coming to us.

It's easy to write those words now, having seen the vision repeatedly fulfilled, but in those early days all we had was that visionary impulse that says, "If you lead many people to the middle of nowhere, it becomes somewhere."

Having a clear vision tells us where we are going to end up, even if it doesn't tell us when or where to expect the twists and turns along the road, or how long the road might be. When circumstances – or stupidity – have us turning to the left or the right, Holy Spirit directed vision is the voice behind us that says *"This is the way. Walk in it."* [65]

With this in mind, as I approach my fiftieth year in 'full time' ministry, I have to admit that one verse is emerging as a 'life scripture' more and more as the years pass.

---

64   Online, see "thekingsschool.info"
65   Isaiah 30:21

And we know that in all things God works for the good of those
who love him,
who have been called according to his purpose. [66]

I appreciate that verse now as I never did as a young man. I
know now, that it really does mean "all things", even the silliest mistake or the most profound foolishness. All things can be
remade into God's original intention; often with added wisdom.
In God's hands, everything can be re-structured to get us there
– eventually.

Perhaps we'll deal with some deeper issues for the directionally
challenged later. For the time being, let me tell you a story of how
God's Spirit took a foolish mistake of mine and turned it into a
miracle. In fact, had I not made the mistake, I probably wouldn't
be referring to this story as a wonderful and life-changing series of
events. And it has everything to do with finding direction.

In the mid 1970s, during our time in Youth With a Mission in the
UK, we went on what was then called the "Middle East Field Trip".
Following the School of Evangelism we were to take a three month
tour through France, Switzerland, Italy, Greece, Crete, Israel,
Egypt, Cyprus, then back to Greece and home again through the
remainder of Western Europe.

What an adventure! And one quite out of the realm of possibil-
ity for these penniless ex-Salvation Army officers and their two
small children, but for the generosity of one of our teachers, Harry
Conn, who donated his honorarium to cover our costs!

As I began to pray about the challenges that lay ahead of us my
mind turned to an elderly couple we had met some years before;
Major and Mrs. Bures (pronounced *boo-resh*). Since their youth,
they had been Salvation Army officers in Czechoslovakia, in a region now called The Czech Republic. They had served until 1950

---

66   Romans 8:28,29 NIV

when The Army was closed down by the Communist authorities. This 'exile' from their public ministry lasted until 1968. Most of that year became known as "The Spring of '68" when reform movements in Czechoslovakia sprang up and out onto the streets and into the media.

It was a glorious time. The fresh scent of freedom was in the air in a way that only proud and sophisticated people such as the Czechs or the Poles and their near neighbors could appreciate after generations of oppressive Soviet domination. In the autumn of '68, despite the pleas of the Czech people to their European neighbors to the West, their 'Spring' was crushed by the invading Russian Army as it came to 'liberate' them from their new-found freedom! The greatest fear of all totalitarian states is a group of intelligent minds accompanied by freedom of choice.

During that Spring of '68 Major and Mrs. Bures traveled to England where they met my parents who were Lt. Colonels in the British Salvation Army. My mother and Mrs. Bures became close friends and on her return to her home in the capital city of Praha, [67] Mrs. Bures would correspond with my mother. The two ladies addressed each other as "My Beloved Sister."

With all this in mind I sat praying about our trip through the Middle East and Southern Europe. 'The Nations' have always been a passion of mine. Even in my childhood, in the motley collection of schools I attended, in which no subject excited me, I was still able to draw a map of the entire Earth. And when I ran out of continents and islands, I'd make a few up – just to fill out The Pacific region a little!

I once conducted an orientation session for a number of American YWAMers. At that time Americans were known to be - shall we say – 'geographically challenged'. Several of them could not identify

---

67   Praha or Prague, then the capital of Czechoslovakia; now the capital of the new Czech Republic

on a map of Europe the nation in which they happened to be sitting! I joked with them that although Abraham stepped out in faith, not knowing where he was going, I assumed at any given point, he knew where he was! [68]

But it wasn't difficult for me to work out that God might want us to take a 'short detour' as we passed the second time through Greece on our return journey and instead of taking the route west, to Italy, strike up north through Communist Yugoslavia, [69] on into Austria and then across the border into Czechoslovakia.

I asked God a simple question. "Lord, should we go to Czechoslovakia to visit Major and Mrs. Bures?" We could encourage them in some way and maybe even meet some other Christians behind the Iron Curtain.

Such a trip could not be taken lightly. The Iron Curtain was a very real and threatening presence in Eastern Europe. Crossing it safely and then maneuvering from one Christian outpost to another was risky business, not only for the visitors but even more so for the hosts who took most of the risk in such ventures.

As I prayed, I decided to write to Mrs. Bures who, by the way, had been a translator in her years of service and spoke English fluently. As I wrote I was walking through the simple facts of the situation. I was writing to our friends in Praha, but I would rather see them, face to face and I wondered if we should visit them. I also acknowledged the fact that Mrs. Bures was a "Sister in the Lord" to my mother, and I was merely that sister's son. Did I have the right to put them and my family at risk?

With these questions in mind I wrote a general greeting. Then I began to think of how to end the letter. Perhaps I could include a

---

68   Hebrews 11:8
69   Through what is now Macedonia, Bosnia & Herzegovina, and Slovenia

concluding statement that Paul had used in one of his epistles. "Now unto Him who is…" No, that wouldn't do. Which Pauline greeting could I use? Then a thought came to mind; "Second John."

I often received ideas like this when God was speaking to me. No Lord, I thought to myself, it's one of Paul's greetings at the end of his letters.

"Second John." It came again. Three times I corrected the voice of the Holy Spirit – as if He didn't know the Scriptures or just what I needed at that moment. In the end I relented and looked it up: Second John, that is, and because I was looking for a suitable ending to my letter I went right to the conclusion of the epistle.

I felt a little silly. Perhaps this was all a fantastic, impractical notion. Here I was, setting pen to paper, wondering whether I should not only write but also visit my mother's 'sister in the Lord'. Then I arrived at Second John, the last verse of which reads:

I have much to write to you, but I do not want to use paper and ink.
Instead, I hope to visit you and talk with you face to face,
so that our joy may be complete.
The children of your chosen sister send their greetings. [70]

Needless to say, we were on our way to Czechoslovakia!

So, there we have it. I must have proven to be a man who had his direction in place. No problems with this guidance. It was as clear as a bell. What's all this about being directionally challenged? Well, the rest of the story comes a few days after we had parted company with the rest of our YWAM group, as they took the Greek ferry to Brindisi, in Italy. We struck out by road to the north.

The journey through Yugoslavia was uneventful, happily so because we had peacefully negotiated our first crossing into Communist

---

70   2 John 12,13 NIV

territory. The next day we were safely across the Czech border and making good time toward the capital city. I was driving. It was then that it hit me. I suddenly realized that I had absolutely no details with me as to where the Bures family lived. Their address sat, carefully transcribed, somewhere in our little apartment on the YWAM base, back in England. I was driving our team towards a massive East European city, governed by an unfriendly Communist authority, and I had no idea where we might be going.

What a fool I felt as I mumbled my explanation and confession to the rest of the team: Jean and our two kids, aged seven and nine, a boy from Sweden, two Texan girls and a young lady from England. They seemed to take the news remarkably well, and we soon found a camp ground on the outskirts of the city and piled into a rough little cabin. The next morning, I explained, the Swede and I would enter the city and.... I wasn't quite sure what came next.

The morning dawned. The ladies did some washing in the crude facilities that displayed the height of communist ingenuity and imagination. They hung the laundry all around the little cabin as the two men set off in the direction of Praha, population 1.2 million people. But hey, we only needed to find two!

Our first stop was in a store which sold books and newspapers. I asked for a map of the city. Some years before, I remembered speaking to a lady who had mentioned she had once lived on a street called 'Londenska' in Prague. I remembered thinking how that sounded to me like 'London Street'.

The lady behind the counter asked "Why you want map?" I told her I wanted to find someone. "Who you want find?" she probed. I wasn't going to reveal that little morsel of information. Again, I asked for a map. Somewhat reluctantly I was handed a large fold-out piece of paper. Upon opening it, I saw four long lines drawn from north, south, east and west. They converged in the middle of the page on an irregular shape, colored in red. Over that shape, in bold black print was the legend: 'Praha'. Obviously, among the various skills of the regime's Information and Publicity Department, cartography was not highly valued, especially when for the benefit of strangers. I handed the map back to the lady. "Thank you. That was a lot of help!" But somehow I felt that my British sarcasm was lost on her.

Nowadays, Praha is crowded with tourists promenading through that beautiful and ancient city, happily taking photos and buying souvenirs. In those days, it was a different story. We immediately attracted too much attention for our comfort. For the next hour we were followed by a man in a raincoat. We knew this simply because he stayed about thirty yards behind us that entire time.

We enacted the most basic of spy mechanisms to spot a 'tail'. When we stopped to look in shop windows he stopped also, keeping his distance behind us. It was a silly strategy because there was nothing of interest in the windows, save great piles of soap powder or some other product in plain grey boxes: another clue to Communist ingenuity.

The most obvious give-away for our unwelcome pursuer was when we paused at one shop, which came at the end of a high brick wall. Sure enough, as we pretended to look in the shop window, he stopped and looked at the brick wall. Perhaps he was as new to this game as we were!

Eventually, we lost our tail. The man in the raincoat gave up, obviously deducing that it was pointless following these two fools who seemed totally lost. As soon as we realized he had gone we looked up and saw a street sign. It read: 'Londýnská'. My 'London Street'. I have since wondered if we were being followed, or whether it was simply an angel, herding us in the right direction!

I recalled that the lady I has spoken to in London, all those years before, had said she knew someone with a Russian sounding name. I thought I remembered it had ended in "ski" and that he had lived in an apartment on the top floor. Could it be that he had lived on "London Street". So, armed with this thought I gave my most affirmative direction of the day. "Let's look along this street and check all the names by the bells. Look for one on the top floor that ends in "ski"… or something like that."

We soon found that Londýnská' was a very long street, stretching a full kilometer all the way from Anglika to Jana Masaryka. And what's more, there were old apartment buildings, several stories high on each side, looking somewhat like the Brown Stones of New York City or the Victorian terraced houses of London. At the entrance to each house was a frame of bells, each one accompanied by the name of the occupant. We began our search, looking for Mr. _____ ski, on the top floor.

Another half an hour went by and I was feeling even more foolish with every passing moment. What an idiot I had been. I had wasted the time, energy and money of my team-mates. I began to imagine the explanations I would make back in England. I would hardly be seen as a trustworthy leader or a man of faith after this one. Then I saw a name tag for "Stranovsky". It was only on the second floor in a five storey building. That's close enough, I thought, so I said "Let's go in here". Amazingly, my Swedish friend concurred, and we climbed the steps to the apartment of Mr. Stranovsky, whoever *he* was!

I knocked at the door, somewhat timidly. After a few seconds, it was opened by an elderly man. He said something which I assumed was a greeting in Czechoslovakian.

"Er…" I began. "We have come from London." Now *that* was imaginative, I thought. But what was I supposed to say? I couldn't reveal to a stranger that I was looking for Mr. and Mrs. Bures, late of The

Salvation Army, a movement banned by the authorities twenty-five years before. "Ah," he said, in perfect English. "Then you will want to come in. Follow me."

Now whether this was a good thing, or bad, we had no idea. But we followed. He led us along a short corridor to a door at the far end. He ushered us through this door and into a small room. We noticed that all three walls were covered with book shelves, full of books. The fourth wall was only big enough to hold the door, the room being no more than six feet square. "Perhaps while you wait, you would like to read a book," he said. "I will return in a moment."

Mr. Stranovsky then left the room and closed the door. We heard his foot steps returning down the corridor. Another door was opened and then closed. Then, silence. What now? Were we in trouble? How could we ever explain our ridiculous behavior? At least, I thought, I am enough of an actor to get us out of this mess without revealing our actual reason for roaming the streets of Praha and knocking on the door of a total stranger.

It was at that point I remembered that our host had suggested I might want to read a book – while I waited. A strange concept! Just how long was he going to be? I scanned the book shelves, only to find that right in line with my eyes, in the middle of a book shelf full of Czech titles, was a slim hard-covered volume. On the spine end of the book was written the title: "The Powers of Salvation Army Officers" by Florence Booth. [71] I took it down from the shelf and held it in my hands.

Within seconds the door opened to reveal Mr. Stranovsky. He smiled as he stood framed in the doorway. "I think I would choose to read this book'" I said, showing him the title on the front cover. "Good," he said, taking the book from me and replacing it on the shelf. "Then I must introduce you to some friends of mine. Their names are Mr. and Mrs. Bures."

71   'The Powers of Salvation Army Officers' by Florence Booth 1914

So, there we were, the recipients of a miracle, participating in a well rehearsed ritual about which we had no previous knowledge, having talked to one man out of 1.2 million, and we were on our way across town to meet the very people who we had travelled across the nations to see. Mr. Stranovsky walked us down the street and toward a tram stop. "When we get in the trolley car, don't speak. It will attract too much attention," he said. Speak? I wanted to shout, I wanted to scream, I was so excited.

How had God done this? He is such a gracious, wonder-working God! And now, thirty years later, out of all the experiences of our Middle East Field Trip, it was the way we found Major and Mrs. Bures that stands out above all the rest; that day when I had no sense of direction and yet found my way.

I have walked through my own experiences and those of friends and colleagues who have really messed up, who after repentance and a submissive heart toward God's dealings, have found themselves right where they had hoped to be before the 'disaster', but simply by a different route. A route they would not and should not have chosen. A route which they know was not God's original intention, but a route that got them there, in the end. I have even heard people admit that it seemed almost better that they came by the way of God's dealings, because of the lessons learned along the path. Could it be that God might not have had the access He desired to deal with the deep inner need, had the right path been chosen?

At this point, we run again to the scripture that says: 'all things work together for good to them that love God, to them who are the called according to his purpose'. [72] But we must follow that up with: 'What shall we say, then? Shall we go on sinning so that grace may increase? By no means! ' [73] It would be somewhat unwise to be careless with our walk just to allow God more room for His redemptive alternatives!

---

72   Romans 8:28 KJV
73   Romans 6:1,2 NIV

Of all the men in the Bible who had challenges with direction, Abraham must come first. Look at this: 'By faith Abraham, when called to go to a place he would later receive as his inheritance, obeyed and went, even though he did not know where he was going.' [74] What was that? He did not know where he was going and yet set out anyway? Now there's a man's man! I wonder if Sarah kept telling him to stop for directions!

Abraham was a true man of vision. God placed in him a certainty, a knowing in the depth of his being, that He was going to establish a people, a city with spiritual rather than physical foundations. He set out to find a city with foundations, whose architect and builder was God. [75]

We have made a few Abraham-like steps in our time. These were times when we knew we were heading somewhere secure, but we also realized that we didn't have the exact address, just a general sense of direction.

By following the inner urging of the Holy Spirit, Jean and I left the comparative security of the denomination of our parents and grandparents. The Salvation Army was all we had ever known from our birth. It was all we had expected to know throughout our ministry, into our retirement, all the way to the moment of our 'Promotion to Glory'. [76]

Our eleven years of Army ministry had been extraordinarily successful. The Army cares for its ministry families. We knew there would not only be a pension for us upon retirement but a comfortable place to live out the rest of our years. We stepped out into what must have looked to others like 'nothing, leading nowhere'. We didn't know where we were going, but it immediately felt more secure than anywhere we had previously been!

---

74   Hebrews 11:8 NIV
75   Hebrews 11:10 NIV
76   'Promoted to Glory' is The Army's description of the death of a Salvation Soldier.

I remember a decisive journey to the United States. We had no notion of it then, but this trip was to open up our entire future. We arrived in New York City's JFK airport. It was late at night. Jean and I bundled our two young kids into a taxi and asked to be taken to the bus station, hoping we wouldn't be just 'taken'. Upon arrival, we sat on our suit cases all night as Kellie and Craig, then 8 and 6, slept in our arms.

The bus pulled out in the early hours, and we were on our way along the NY Thruway toward Buffalo. It made a scheduled stop in Syracuse somewhere around lunch time, although to the British time-clocks in our heads it was already evening. We bought a plate of fried eggs and some toast. Jean and I watched as the kids ate it gratefully. On the way back to the bus we passed a candy machine. I dropped a couple of coins in, and we had a chocolate bar for the kids to snack on, the rest of the way. As the coins jingled their way down to the belly of the machine I realized I had just let go of my last bit of money.

I sat thinking about this for the remaining hours of the journey, but I didn't admit it until we were walking down the aisle of the bus at the Buffalo terminal. "We don't even have a dime to put in the phone to tell them we're here." I said. At this, Kellie suddenly turned around and went back down the aisle to the area near her seat where she began poking her little-girl fingers down the backs of the seats. Within seconds, she returned with one dime. We disembarked, put our dime in a pay-phone, called our hosts, they came to meet us, and our future opened up before us.

Just like the coin Peter found in the mouth of a fish, our dime was God's supply to get us from where we were to where we needed to be. [77]

I had a friend who, by the time I met him, was a distinguished ministry man in his senior years. But as a mere boy he had trained as a U.S. Army Air Corps navigator during the closing months of the Second World War. He told me of his first trip across the Atlantic. After some hours, they had spotted land. "Where are we?" demanded his captain. My friend gulped down the nerves that threatened to choke his answer. He checked the reference lines he'd drawn on his charts and said: "It could be Iceland, or it could be Spain, but I think it's Ireland!"

People of vision know where they are going. They just don't always know the exact address or the ETA. They are marked with what, to others, seems like an annoying self-assurance that flies in the face of reason and logic, but in reality, it is the fire that sparks the zeal in those without the vision. It fans the flame of passion that keeps others going toward that 'place'. And upon arrival, every demon in Hell shudders at the realization that God's people have once more attained a position and a place they didn't deserve, having walked along a path they didn't know.

Have you ever wondered what they'll put on your grave stone? How about: "Here lies _____ , who was severely directionally challenged, but who got there just the same, and took a host of others along for the ride!"

8

Dumb and Loving It!

"Woe to me!" I cried. "I am ruined! For I am a man of unclean lips, and I live among a people of unclean lips, and my eyes have seen the King, the LORD Almighty." [78]

For 'ruined', read the Hebrew *damah:* to be dumb, to fall silent. [79]

When it comes to my understanding of Heaven, I grew up on a consistent diet which did not give me much hope of an interesting existence 'on the other side'. So far as I could make, out we were to be preoccupied with walking on streets of gold - that is when we weren't sitting on clouds singing worship songs, no doubt while playing extremely heavy harps; heavy, because they were to be made of the same stuff as the streets.

More recent years saw me reading a little of the testimonies of one or two preachers who claim to have been up to Heaven, not for keeps, but just for a look-see! Again I was deeply suspicious as one

---

78   Isaiah 6:5 NIV
79   Strong's words: OT 1820

after another described nothing more than a series of human-sized concepts. One man even said that Heaven's occupants were sitting in rows having a meeting. Pews in Heaven? Give me a break!

As years went by and I began preaching, I enjoyed creating a picture of what our hereafter could look like. I theorized that the lights in the universe had been switched off at the fall of mankind, but after the Second Coming we would have full access, once more, to all of creation. We would then be commissioned to exciting adventures, repopulating the exotic fantastical realms of God's imagination.

This sort of picture seemed to be more in tune with what I had learned of God's creative energy. My boyhood images of angels sitting on clouds playing ten-string lyres were relegated back to their place sitting atop tombstones, where they belonged. Then something happened, not in my imagination but in real life and real time; something that changed my expectation of Heaven, completely.

In the early 1990s, our family moved down to Virginia for a year. By now Kellie was married, and we had adopted our third child, John William, out of Bogotá, Colombia. So it was Craig, Jongie, Jean and me, in the capitol of the Old Confederacy.

Back in New York our church had been experiencing some extraordinary things. Meetings were being interrupted by waves of laughter, which swept through the congregation, often when there was nothing funny going on. It seemed to all concerned that 'the joy of the Lord' was visiting His Church. I was all for that! It reminded me of the time when 'the priests could not perform their service because of the cloud, for the glory of the LORD filled the temple of God.' [80]

Each month we would travel north to minister at two of the churches we had planted and into which we had some apostolic input:

80   2 Chronicles 5:14 NIV

First Church of Granville, on the border of New York and Vermont, and Church of the Nations in Lake Luzerne. One Sunday evening we sat with the elders of Church of The Nations as they gathered in the home of Derek and Mary Jane Bevan, who had taken over as pastors of COTN. We had been walking through a hurtful and terrible time in our ministry and these faithful friends gathered around us in friendship and support.

The evening started innocently enough. A few choruses in worship were augmented by some words of testimony, observation and encouragement - nothing out of the ordinary. Then, without warning or obvious reason these respectable sincere people began breaking into laughter. It seemed to start opposite the couch where Jean and I sat, it then moved from seat to seat, along the line of those sitting facing us. At the other end of the couch sat a friend and his wife, the two ladies sitting together in between us men. The laughter came around the corner at the end of the room and caught up with my friend at the other end of our couch.

I remember thinking how funny it would be to see it catch my friend's wife and then continue on to Jean, who sat to my right. But no such luck! It seemed to jump the two ladies, and – you've guessed – it fell on me, like a bolt of friendly lightening. I then had an impression in my mind – a suggestion, really. "You don't have to stay on the sofa." I knew it was an implicit word to me to slide off the edge of my seat and drop to my knees on the carpet in front of me. In fact, a second 'word' came to me as I began to move. "It's on the carpet!"

As soon as my knees touched down on that carpet, it began; waves of laughter and tears, laughter and tears, laughter and tears. I couldn't make out which had the ascendency. I collapsed in a heap then began rolling around the room, helpless to stop myself. Laughing, crying, groaning... and rolling! Yes, I had officially become a 'Holy Roller'.

From time to time, I would attempt to control myself. Of course the rest of the occupants in the room now had something legitimate to laugh at and the mirth became uncontrollable, even more so when I saw that my friend from the other end of the sofa was also on the carpet, rolling a little behind me, but somewhat faster! That meant that every so often he overtook me, and I mean "over" took. He rolled right on top of me, giving me a glimpse of his round face roaring in laughter down at mine, then he went ahead, on his next lap.

This went on for about forty minutes. I knew I was being healed of something deep inside me. I cannot explain it, but something was being drawn out of me with every burst of laughter and every squeezed-out tear. Moment by moment I felt I was being drawn closer and closer to my Healer.

Then the room went quiet. I stopped my progress at one end of the carpet, and I lay there, I am told, for another twenty minutes; the apostle of the ministry, the founder of the church, the senior pastor; lying like a child at the feet of the other leaders.

It was then that something came on me, the like of which I had never experienced before. The presence of God came into the room and fell on me like a blanket. I lay before the Face of God. Deep within me, I knew that I was not only loved, I was *being* loved. Love and acceptance were being poured into me. The room was silent yet volumes were being spoken into my being. To this day I struggle to find words to describe the experience without dissolving into tears.

Then came a clear and simple revelation which affected my picture of Heaven – you remember, that active adventurous picture I had developed, which sounded more like an episode of Star Wars than Sunday School. Ever since then it has affected my walk here on Earth, because I realized I was literally in the presence of God.

I dared not say anything. I *would* not say anything. I didn't *want* to say anything or do anything. And yet I knew that I was absolutely, totally, completely fulfilled. I knew, in that moment, that I had no need for anything or even anyone else, because Jesus was there - right there - and He was everything.

I reassessed my expectation of Heaven. With Jesus present, I would have no need of adventures, discoveries or intergalactic travel. He is and will be everything. After all, Jesus is 'before all things, and in him all things hold together.' [81] 'He is the image of the invisible God, the firstborn over all creation.' [82] He is everything. 'Christ is all, and is in all.' [83]

I have little doubt that God will have us involved in all sorts of creative activities throughout our eternity with Him, but they will have a marked difference from man-made adventures here on Earth. In heaven, we will not feel obliged to seek challenge and adventure merely to fulfill ourselves or meet some need for self-awareness or value. All of that will be met fully, in Jesus. In Heaven, we will be involved in activity simply as an expression of our complete satisfaction with Him. But wait – isn't that how it's supposed to be down here, as we walk daily in His presence?

Isn't it amazing that God, who is the Omnipresent [84]– who is everywhere, all the time – may still make His presence felt in more noticeable ways, just to delight His children?

We speak of meetings and times of worship by saying "God was really there." I have known times when He has manifested His presence in a particular part of the meeting place, even to the point that a section of the crowd elsewhere in the auditorium rushed over to the other side to get in on the experience of His presence!

81   Colossians 1:17 NIV
82   Colossians 1:15,16 NIV
83   Colossians 3:11 NIV
84   Omnipresent = 'Infinite in presence' – see Jeremiah 23:24; 1 Kings 8:27; Psalm 139:7-10; Prov. 15:3

Sadly there are other times when the Omnipresent will withdraw His presence – or, more accurately, He will lift the awareness of His presence. Adam discovered this personally when he was separated from His creator. [85] His son Cain, whose resentful anger seduced him to sin, said that his punishment was "…more than I can bear. Today you are driving me from the land and I will be hidden from your presence." [86]

David was aware of the blessing of God's presence which is why he so feared it being removed. He wrote: 'Do not cast me from your presence or take your Holy Spirit from me." [87]

At a glance, it seems that the presence of God should be the everyday climate of the believer, but it is much more than that. Moses showed a profound understanding of the effect and influence of God's presence when he said: "If your Presence does not go with us, do not send us up from here." That was his assessment; that God's presence should be the climate and context of the people of God. But his understanding went farther. He continued: "How will anyone know that you are pleased with me and with your people unless you go with us?" In other words, our significance and value is marked only by the God's presence.

Next he spoke a line that few of us have appreciated to the full: "What else will distinguish me and your people from all the other people on the face of the earth?" [88] Moses had learned that there is only one thing that distinguishes the believer from the lost. It is not our behavior. The ungodly can affect good behavior, even if only for the sake of self preservation. It is not by our church buildings, our worship bands or our ability to "match" the world in any way. There are more magnificent buildings just around the corner and the style of contemporary worship is still playing catch-up

---

85   Genesis 3:23,24
86   Genesis 4:14 NIV
87   Psalm 51:11,12 NIV
88   Exodus 33:15,16 NIV

with the world's music. No! The distinguishing factor, which Moses states prophetically will be noticeable to the world, will be the fact that God is manifesting His presence in, around and through His people, in a manner which the world will recognize but never be able to replicate.

From what I have learned about God's presence – which you will recall has been more than enough to satisfy me – I have seen that He manifests this experience differently to one person than to another. He is personal about His presence. He is a relational being who cares more about developing His relationships than manifesting His power. To one person, a meeting with God brings indescribable peace, to another, unspeakable joy, while to some, unbearable awe.

Charles Grandison Finney was a lawyer-turned-preacher whom God used to quicken much of America's Second Great Awakening. He testified to a profound meeting with God in the offices of his law firm. He told of waves of love coursing over him time and again, until he cried out to God to stop!

In his memoirs Finney writes: "...as I turned and was about to take a seat by the fire, I received a mighty baptism of the Holy Spirit. Without any expectation of it, without ever having the thought in my mind that there was any such thing for me, without any memory of ever hearing the thing mentioned by any person in the world, the Holy Spirit descended upon me in a manner that seemed to go through me, body and soul. I could feel the impression, like a wave of electricity, going through and through me. Indeed it seemed to come in waves of liquid love, for I could not express it in any other way. It seemed like the very breath of God. I can remember distinctly that it seemed to fan me, like immense wings. No words can express the wonderful love that was spread abroad in my heart. I wept aloud with joy and love. I literally bellowed out the unspeakable overflow of my heart. These waves came over me, and over me, and over me, one after the other, until I remember crying out. "I shall die if these waves continue to pass over me." I said. "Lord, I cannot bear any more," yet I had no fear of death. [89]

It's interesting to see that God chose to fill the emotions of this man who for years had been known for his academic and legal ability. To this day, he is renowned for his brilliance in systematic teaching, yet, when meeting a man with such a mind, God chose to fill his emotions to overflowing. Perhaps God knows what academics really need!

My meeting with God, on the carpet of my friend's house, came during one of the most hurtful times in my life. For years, we had developed relationships with churches and leaders in various parts of the world. We had changed the name of our local church to match the vision in our hearts and the growing network of relationships we enjoyed.

Many other churches in the network followed suit, changing their names to match the vision, and the network itself adopted the name I had chosen for our church. Locally, the 120 acres of prime Adirondack land had become the center for ministry schools, the Service Corps [90] and international summer camps. It was identified as the 'international center' of the network. Personnel from other countries started moving in and Jean and I prepared for the future by phasing out of our immediate pastoral responsibilities by handing over to our faithful friends.

However, life in the Adirondacks did not suit some of the leaders who had migrated in. Within months of their arrival, new 'guidance' came along, which led key members of the team off to other parts of the States. Ours was no longer to be the interna-

---

89   Autobiography of Charles G. Finney; The Life Story of America's Greatest Evangelist--In His Own Words by Charles G. Finney. ISBN13: 9780764201561

90   Now known as Service International

tional center. The direction which an entire international team had seen as God's guidance was now in question. Plans changed. We were left, confused, hurt, and out of a job!

All this was simply the outcome of bad planning, questionable guidance, poor communication and an unhealthy degree of inse-curity – but all mixed, I choose to believe, with sincerity and good intentions, gone astray.

For a year or so we tried to make the best of it. We reminded our-selves that "As they pass through the Valley of Baca, they make it a place of springs; the autumn rains also cover it with pools. They go from strength to strength." [91] After all, there's a reason why Baca was a good place to dig wells and find springs. As the name implied, it was saturated with tears. [92]

Our hurts were far too close to the surface to ignore. The work we had put into the previous fifteen years of ministry all but evapo-rated. Some who had walked closely with us seemed to lose our address and phone number. So it was in that state of mind and heart that we returned to the faithful bunch of leaders in our home church. They were as confused as we were when looking at the results of the previous months, but that didn't change their com-mitment and love toward us.

So it was that we met to worship, that Sunday evening, and I had my time on the carpet, in the presence of God. Did He come in judgment? Was He determined to set me straight? No, He came with acceptance, approval, affirmation. In fact, He came with just what I needed. Typical!

I have always enjoyed a keen sense of God's presence and, con-sequently, I usually know when He's conspicuously absent! It might be of the spirit, or maybe just in my Celtic blood-line. In his book

91   Psalm 84:6,7 NIV
92   Baka' - Strong's OT word No. 1056, from OT:1058, 'weeping'.

'The Celtic Way', Ian Bradley writes: The Celts felt the presence of Christ almost physically woven around their lives. They were conscious of being encircled by him, upheld by him and encompassed by him. This almost tangible experience of Jesus as a companion next to you, a guest in your house, a physical presence in your life was perhaps the most striking way in which the Celts expressed their overwhelming sense of the divine presence. [93]

Not surprisingly the Celtic Christians, who predated most nations in their obedience to Christ [94] often sensed God's presence in the material world around them, not unlike their pantheistic forbears who had literally worshiped the creation. Sometimes I wonder whether those Pagan Pantheists were closer to the truth than many an unseeing and unfeeling modern Christian. After all, it was Paul who said: 'since the creation of the world God's invisible qualities — his eternal power and divine nature — have been clearly seen, being understood from what has been made, so that men are without excuse.' [95]

A young Celt who was born in 'The Fort of The Britons', [96] was taken as a slave by his Celtic neighbors to the west. He escaped and somehow got to Rome where God called him back to the land of his slave masters. Padraigh was his name; later to be known as St. Patrick, Patron Saint of Ireland. He wrote this verse about God's wonderful presence in everything. It's called 'Patrick's Breastplate'.

Christ be with me, Christ within me, Christ behind me,
Christ before me, Christ beside me, Christ to win me,
Christ to comfort and restore me, Christ beneath me, Christ above me,
Christ in quiet, Christ in danger, Christ in hearts of all that love me,
Christ in mouth of friend or stranger.

93   p. 33 'The Celtic Way' by Ian Bradley (New Edition) Published 2003 by Darton, Longman & Todd Ltd.

94   Tertullian of Carthage (born 160 A.D)wrote of the Celtic "regions of the Britons inaccessible to the Romans but subject to Christ."

95   Romans 1:20 NIV

96   Being translated: 'Dumbarton' a Scottish town at the mouth of the Clyde.

When walking on the Celtic Isle of Iona during this 21st Century, I passed a spot on a path at which I felt a surge of 'something' that caught my breath and drew me to tears. Later that day I passed over the same path once more and experienced the same reaction, even though I stood close to all the multi-national tourists, clicking their cameras at the 14th Century abbey, which is almost 'contemporary' on that ancient isle. Who knows what had happened on that spot, so many centuries before? But there was still a 'presence' there.

Becoming sensitive to God's presence also comes in handy when you need to identify when He has quit the scene. In the late 1980s Jean and I led a group of church leaders to view a property which seemed ideal for our International Ministry School. It had the required accommodation, rooms for lectures and meetings, a commercial kitchen and more than adequate dining facilities. The front door even opened up onto the first tee of the local golf course! What more could we want?

After several minutes of walking around the place, admiring all its features, we were met by Jean, who declared: "There's a monster in the basement!"

We knew she wasn't simply reacting to some childish fear. We had always enjoyed joking with children about their fears of 'monsters under the bed' or 'in the closet' assuring them that if there really was a monster in the house, it couldn't be all that scary if it was hiding in the closet. "The really scary ones" we assured them, "would be sitting in your Dad's Lay-z-boy, drinking his coffee and playing with the TV remote!

This was no joke. We knew immediately that Jean's discernment saw something lurking beneath the surface of that property, and we were to have nothing to do with it, despite all its obvious attributes. In time, we discovered that the property had numerous liens placed on it and unresolved disputes dating back some years

– and most of them coming from a secret society which had once owned the place! Those who are sensitive to God's presence are immediately aware of His absence.

When it comes to appreciating the impact of God's presence, I love Isaiah's testimony. He caught a revelation of the reality of God's presence through a vision that held nothing of the peaceful healing which He had allowed me on that carpet. I smile (sympathetically) at those who say "When I get to Heaven, I'm going to walk right up and ask God….." and then they trot out their latest question, which will no doubt confound the Almighty! No. When we check out Isaiah's experience we catch a glimpse at the reality of His *actual* presence.

"In the year that King Uzziah died," he begins "I saw the Lord seated on a throne, high and exalted, and the train of his robe filled the temple. Above him were seraphs, each with six wings: With two wings they covered their faces, with two they covered their feet, and with two they were flying. And they were calling to one another: "Holy, holy, holy is the Lord Almighty; the whole earth is full of his glory." At the sound of their voices the doorposts and thresholds shook and the temple was filled with smoke." [97]

OK! So now we have something of the picture. God, enthroned. Awesome Seraphs flying around Him with voices that shook the foundations! Then Isaiah testifies to a perfectly reasonable response: "Woe to me!" He cried. "I am ruined!"

That word 'ruined' says it all. The King James Version uses the term 'undone'. The original word is *damah*. It means to perish; to be confounded; to be reduced to silence. I like the Strong's translation: 'I was left dumb'. [98]

---

97   Isaiah 6:1-5 NIV

98   Strong's word number 1820 – to be dumb or silent; hence to fail or perish.

If Isaiah had been privileged to have been educated in Liverpool, rather than in the upper classes of Jerusalem, he might have said, "I was gob-smacked!" It means the same thing.

I don't pretend to be an Isaiah, but I have been prophetic from time to time, even to the extent that I know the tongue of the prophet can be sharp. A prophet's feelings are easily aroused and his way with words can be caustic, critical, even cynical or sarcastic. Perhaps God saw that in Isaiah. Maybe that was what needed to be dealt with during his meeting with God by that 'coal off the altar'. [99]

The glimpse given to Isaiah must have changed him for ever, and it certainly put a halter on his mouth and a bit between his lips. From that day on, Isaiah knew he would be better off dumb than speaking his own brand of judgment.

I have used words all my life. I love language. I grew up in a nation that excelled in playing with words. But of all the things by which I have been marked, most of all I treasure the moments when I have been struck dumb – in His presence.

99   Isaiah 6:6,7

9

Getting Smaller Every Day

I sometimes think that God called me to the United States and set me in leadership as something of a joke on American society. Inhabitants of the New World have seldom had to deal with an authoritative voice which comes from somewhere close to their belt buckle.

I am no midget. I outgrew my gene pool by a mile or so, but that still leaves me hovering around 5' 6". My father, who was a giant of a man in every respect other than his physical stature, was a few inches shy of my lofty height. I towered over my mother, and my sisters are similarly vertically challenged. Size never seemed to matter much in our family. The dynamic of that man and those three ladies I just mentioned is the main reason. But on American standards, I am a small man, and in America, size matters.

Americans have a thing about height. Truthfully I never felt small until I came to the United States. I grew up in Post War Britain where the starvation rations of the 1940s left us thinking more about survival than any other physical achievement.

I was only a little below the average size of my mates in school, although stronger and faster than most. In my Rugby days in Kent, I was the scrappy scrum half or the nippy winger. As a soccer player I was naturally delighted at the sight of some big fellas trundling onto the field with the opposing team. No doubt they would prove to be ponderous and easily grounded by a player with a lower center of gravity, and my center was only slightly above 'ground zero'. We usually left the big guys in our dust, or in our slush, frost or snow, as the case may be in England's national sport which begins in August and finds its climax the following May!

On Saturday afternoons in Liverpool in the 1950s there was nothing quite so enjoyable as watching Scottish International Bobby Collins playing for Everton. Running around, and sometimes into the opposition, his 5' 3" frame and size 3 boots would leave behind many a crunching tackle on a larger defender, like a calling card that would be remembered for several days after the final whistle.

Even when I become an old man (which at 65, I should have attained by now, but which still seems illusive) I will fondly recall the day our college team played the London City Police. After ten minutes, and almost as many goals which left the hulking police goalie flat footed, their captain approached us with a request to 'slow it down a bit'. He looked down at me. "It's only a friendly," he pleaded.

Those big policemen would have been more at home in these United States, where big boys – often fat and unfit boys – can find a place on the line in the local football team. American Football, that is; that's the game which is played mostly with the hands and not the feet. Most of the players have little expectation of ever actually touching the ball, in fact the coach might tell some of his biggest guys to stay away from it! So for them, "foot" and "ball" are simply mysterious statements of faith.

We once had a giant of a kid in our King's School. Very few students were kinder or gentler than this boy who was closer to seven feet tall than six, even when still in High School. Not only was he tall, he was big with it; in fact, too big. This boy received a letter from a College Football coach in a neighboring state. It started: "Dear _____, an athlete such as yourself...." It continued with promises of a place on the team and a scholarship. The poor boy could hardly move; he was so big. I guess that made the coach even more excited. But in his homeland that's what they called him – an athlete.

A four year college football player sat down with him one day. "In their eyes" he said, "you're a big piece of meat, and you'll be just fine until they find a bigger piece. Then, you might be just so much meat on the shelf." That might not have been the best advice for every big kid, but for this boy, it was. He was too often defined by his size. But to those of us who knew him, we valued him for so much more.

Coming to America I faced a challenge. Not only is it impossible for me to find pants that fit the length of my legs or jackets with the correct sleeve length, but I have to deal with the misconception that size is a character quality to be praised rather than a natural attribute which is genetic and inevitable. There seems to be no understanding that achieving a certain height is no more praiseworthy than keeping oneself small.

I have discovered that leaders, especially in the political realm, are often chosen and followed passionately because of their physical attributes as highly as anything else - and especially because of their height. The few brave women who enter politics have found that height, gestures, facial expressions and gait often far outweigh the importance of their intelligence, their ideas or their ability. How many times have I sat watching the earliest rounds of a Primary Election for the presidency of the United States, only to come to the conclusion that candidate nos. 3 and 5 have the best ideas and the sharpest intellect, but they don't stand a chance? They just don't look right! This is not only sad, it's dangerous!

Jesse "The Body" Ventura, the one-time wrestler who became the governor of Minnesota, once said: "People need someone to look up to and I'm six foot four." Now that might not be the most philo-sophical thing a U.S. Governor has ever said, but even as a joke, it shows a trend.

I recall a good Christian lady once commenting on a gospel film she had just watched. She had enjoyed it, but for one flaw. She was upset that one or two of the disciples had been depicted as being taller than Jesus! "How could they *do* that!" she exclaimed. So I told her a story.

When I was a teen back in England, I went with some of my friends to a 'stately home' near Liverpool in the town of Speke. The bus ride there was memorable in that a man stood up in the front and shouted to the passengers: "Hush, this bus is going to Speke!" Only in Liverpool!

Upon arrival at the site, we met with a guide who took us around the halls of this grand old pile. He pointed out some suits of armor that stood like silent sentinels along a hallway. Noticing the height of the suits of armor, one of our group noted that the knights must have been very small men. "That's how you know it's the genuine article" said the guide, "and not some modern replica. People in those days were generally much smaller than modern man."

Back to my friend who was reviewing the gospel movie. "What's that to do with the actor portraying Jesus?" she asked. "Well" I countered. "If men in the Middle Ages were smaller than their 21st Century counterparts, imagine how small Jesus might be!" "Wouldn't it be funny," I continued, "If we get to Heaven only to find the Lord of Lords is four foot nine! We'd have to get on our knees to worship Him." What a novel concept!

Of course, all the 'pieces of the cross' of Christ which have been gathered and venerated at various basilicas around Europe, put together, would measure a mile or so, so who knows how big Jesus must have been – according to that logic!

Being noticed, affirmed, followed, idolized, or even rejected because of one's size is a form of bigotry. And it's just silly. In his lecture on cross cultural ministry Loren Cunningham [100] once said: "Prejudice is to judge a person on the basis of an attribute over which they have no control." There is nothing we can do about our race, our hair color (although some have found a surface solution to that one) or our size, although we should probably list that one as 'height', because we Americans have plenty we could do about our other vital statistics.

Judging someone by an uncontrollable physical attribute makes for an unhealthy lack of self worth. Whenever a person is praised for something for which they know they had little responsibility, it may cause an opportunity for the enemy to devalue that person in their thought life. "You see? They only love you because you are so tall!" Conversely, when someone is rejected for the same unfounded reason, the enemy's opportunity is just as great, if not greater.

Poor young King Saul! He is a classic example of this dilemma. His problems began some time before he was appointed as King over Israel, when the leaders of the nation approached the Prophet Samuel. This contingent had not yet heard the scripture that states: "For God so loved the world that He did not send a committee!" They thought they had the collective wisdom to appeal to the old prophet. "You are old," they said, "and your sons do not walk in your ways; now appoint a king to lead us, such as all the other nations have." [101]

---

100   Loren Cunningham - The founder of Youth With A Mission
101   1 Samuel 8:5 NIV

It doesn't take much discernment to notice that things had started to go wrong, from the outset. "Such as all the other nations have"? Why would Israel even consider wanting to be like "all the other nations"? The very essence of their existence was based on their Hebrew-ish-ness. They had 'come over' from nowhere. They were once 'not a people', but now, they were the people of God. Their identity was not of their own making, and it certainly would not be enhanced by becoming more like everyone else!

However, God gave them exactly what they asked for, He tends to do that to rebellious people. He always will. Hell itself is not a place God willingly sets people into, but rather a place he brokenheartedly allows people to enter of their own free will – allowing them exactly what they've requested all their lives – absence from Him.

God's response to Israel's request was: King Saul, a young man with a particular attribute which made him more than attractive to the eyes of the beholders. He was taller than everyone else. [102]

At the time of his coronation the people gathered, wild with excitement and anticipation. On this great day, they could tell their grandchildren, God made us "like all the other nations"! The crowds of elders gathered, representing tribes, clans and families throughout Israel. A throne was prepared. Samuel had a horn of oil ready for the anointing, but the new king was nowhere to be found.

At this point, I want to make a case for the kid who was taller than anyone else in the nation. I truly believe – even from my position 5' 6" from terra firma, that Saul was suffering from the anxiety of being judged for his size – an attribute about which he could do nothing – and not for his character, for which he was solely responsible. On the day of his coronation, he hid himself away, and that's not easy for a kid who was born for basketball, about three thousand years before the game was invented!

102   1 Samuel 9:2

The people decided to inquire of the Lord. It was a little late in the day to be doing this, but they did so, just the same. Now they were asking God where their king might be – a question to which God alone knew the answer.

"So they inquired further of the LORD, "Has the man come here yet?" And the LORD said, "Yes, he has hidden himself among the baggage." They ran and brought him out, and as he stood among the people he was a head taller than any of the others. Samuel said to all the people, "Do you see the man the LORD has chosen? There is no one like him among all the people." [103]

Perhaps someone should have answered, "Well, let's think about this for a second. He was *hiding*... before his coronation!?" But no-one had the fortitude to do so, so they all shouted: "Long live the king!"

Being head and shoulders above the rest of the nation was not the wisest or the most comfortable position for a king at that time in history. Those were the days when kings were propped up in chariots and paraded *in front* of their armies. Even a novice archer had a reasonable shot at toppling the monarch, especially if he was the largest target on the field of battle! And it was not the wisest move from another point of view. Inside the tallest man of all there was a little boy, crying to be recognized for who and what he really was.

Later in the sad life of Saul, he compromised his position of authority, and not for the first time, showed his fear of man – even those subordinate to him. So God led the prophet Samuel to say this to him. "Although you were once small in your own eyes, did you not become the head of the tribes of Israel? The LORD anointed you king over Israel". [104]

---

103   1 Samuel 10:22-24 NIV
104   1 Samuel 15:17 NIV

Think of it — head and shoulders over everyone in the nation, yet small in his own eyes.

People around us will constantly attempt to see us according to the external. How tall or how short we might be. This works against an important attribute which the Spirit of God is working to perfect in us all. It is humility.

Humility is being willing to be known for who and what we really are, strengths and weaknesses. As we walk in humility, we allow people to see the real person inside. But if they judge us to be something else, on the basis of some unavoidable attribute, which shows only the façade of our existence, then at least we can walk in humility, refusing the accolade, or the demotion that comes from superficial judgments.

It was Micah who said: "the LORD has already told you what is good, and this is what he requires: to do what is right, to love mercy, and to walk humbly with your God. [105]

It's not so hard to walk humbly before God. We know that He sees us as we really are. He is not swayed by our size, or lack thereof. The more difficult task is to walk humbly before our fellow men, who so often judge us by a set of values way below God's.

When Samuel was looking around for Saul's successor, and still assuming God would supply a king "like all the other nations", God set him straight by saying, of one handsome delegate: "Do not consider his appearance or his height, for I have rejected him. The LORD does not look at the things man looks at. Man looks at the outward appearance, but the LORD looks at the heart." [106]

---

105   Micah 6:8 NLT
106   1 Samuel 16:7 NIV

So, to walk humbly before our God is one thing, but to walk out our humility in the company of our fellow humans takes a little more perseverance.

I find very few things more endearing than a giant of a man who is properly "little" inside. My friend John Dean is such a man - a prophet and a father in the faith to a generation or two of leaders and a colleague of mine on one of the Coordinating Teams of Alliance International Ministries. "Big John" comes from Texas, and you can tell that from about a mile off! He has all the physical attributes that help you to understand the meaning of "Don't mess with Texas".

It would be so easy for him to simply rest back in his natural attributes. A hug from Big John feels different than one from someone of smaller stature. He enters a room and immediately fills it – in more ways than one! People will naturally (and that's the right word) see him as a man of authority, because of his size, but if he's a Saul on the outside, he's a David in his heart. He seems willing only to take up the room that God appoints for him in any given situation.

I have not met many men who are more submissive than John to the godly authority around him. One of his favorite teachings is on a person's 'Measure of Rule', the place inside the boundaries which God has set on our ministry or responsibility and our respect for those places in the lives and ministries of others.

I've seen plenty of preachers who strut their stuff up on stage, enjoying the largeness of their physical presence. I've also seen a few little Napoleons desperate to compensate for their perceived 'lack'. Then there are those, of whatever physical dimension, who are small inside, and getting smaller every day; walking in humility; leaving room for the power of God.

10
On Crutches

I enjoy it when people say "This is my life's verse." They find one section of scripture that seems to sum it all up, for them. That isn't oversimplifying the matter; it's defining it simply, but with profound meaning. For me there is not necessarily a single verse or passage, unless it is these verses from Paul's first letter to the church in Corinth.

> Brothers, think of what you were when you were called.
> Not many of you were wise by human standards;
> not many were influential;
> not many were of noble birth.
> But God chose the foolish things of the world to shame the wise;
> God chose the weak things of the world to shame the strong.
> He chose the lowly things of this world and the despised things —
> and the things that are not — to nullify the things that are,
> so that no one may boast before him. [107]

For me, that verse sums up the total effect of God's marks on my life. It states that if anything of value has been seen or experienced

---
107   1 Corinthians 1:26-29 NIV

by myself, or by those with whom I have come in contact, then it really has to have been of God. It also speaks into what I believe has become my life's theme: the difference between gifting and character.

If you've persisted through this book it must be obvious to you by now that I have a "thing" about that difference. Character is the fruit of the responses we make to God's marks, His dealings in our lives. Just as wisdom is the proper use of knowledge, and should never be confused, one with the other, so character is the proper context of our gifts.

It was only in the second lengthy chapter of my ministry, namely the last thirty-five years that this understanding took root. It became the answer to why I was so concerned about the first chapter – my beginnings in ministry.

During those early years, I was given the maximum possible attention, acceptance, adulation and affirmation. That might not sound like a problem to you, but if those things are heaped on a person for the wrong reasons, the whole affair becomes inordinate - that which is not ordained. If a thing is not ordained it is not blessed - and if not blessed, it is not fed by grace and will soon run dry.

You will recall my description of a time when God dealt with the hypocrisy in my life and - without shedding one ounce of personal responsibility - I have come to realize that within all the darkness of that period, I was also reacting to the hypocrisy of my environment.

If a person is told he is "great" he has only a few possible responses. He may believe his own publicity and live in narcissistic deception, he may totally refuse the accolade and hate himself for the lie he is living, or he may walk in humility and give the glory to God. This is why so many celebrities struggle with fame and become self-destructive.

I recall a friend telling me of a story he had witnessed. A famous preacher was invited onto a late night TV show. One of his fellow guests was a well known star of the day who was about to enter into yet another marriage, having failed at several previous attempts. During the course of the broadcast, the celebrity made some crude jokes, at the expense of his latest fiancé, who sat out in the Green Room. He was determined to show the audience that he was on top of his world and had a laugh a minute to prove it.

Eventually, the preacher got a word in. He said: "If that's the case, why do you cry yourself to sleep every night?" An awkward silence was broken by the laughter of the audience, thinking it was just another joke.

After the show, the preacher and his wife were leaving by the stage door when the celebrity called out to them from inside his limousine, and they accepted a lift back to their hotel. When they were seated inside the vehicle, the celebrity looked anxiously over to the preacher and said: "Tell me, how you knew that I cry myself to sleep every night?"

Here was yet another man who knew that, in comparison to the reality of his inner life; the applause and the laughter were as hollow as the place in which he feared he would probably end up.

He was an outcome of a society which is determined to value giftedness above character. The tragedy is this: the Church – the Body of Christ – has the same tendency toward its celebrities. The gullibility of present day Christians in flocking after the gifted is frightening. It is serious enough to assume that God might soon limit His release of the Gifts!

Now, I am a "gift" man. I love the release of the gifts of the Spirit, but even after years of being led by the Holy Spirit and of witnessing the power of His visitation on people's lives, I would still give a thousand gifted people for one or two who showed godly character.

I remember a national leader in The Salvation Army engaging me in conversation shortly after I had been baptized in the Holy Spirit. He inquired as to how the wonderful things that had happened in my life had come about. "I want you to know that we all see a different Bill", he said. "But with all this emphasis on the Gifts, just never lose sight of the Fruits of the Spirit also". I saw that as an attempt to deflect me away from the power of the Spiritual Gifts or to dilute my new-found experience. Now, however, I say, "Amen".

What is it that compels us to follow after gifted people as if by some means they had acquired the gift through their own merit? This is the crux of the matter. Earlier in this book I stated that the biblical term for 'gift' and 'grace' is one and the same. [108] If a person or a crowd ever gives so much as the impression that a gift is a badge of merit for which someone deserves credit, then it becomes a total denial of grace.

The best way I have found for describing the gifts of grace is to call them 'crutches'. A crutch is a tool, a means by which someone can get to a place to which they could not attain without its help. Nobody boasts about their crutches. "Hey, you see my crutches? Bet you wish you had at least one like mine!" Nobody lines up to see a guy with a crutch! Very few would travel to a seminar or conference on the strength of the crutches used by the speaker. A crutch is not a sign of ability. Rather, it's the sign of a disability.

Where does that leave the 'multi-gifted' person? I have been described as "multi-gifted". Music, drama, preaching, teaching, writing, composing, leadership, the prophetic, the apostolic, and if my mother was still alive I'm sure she could add a few more! But think of the multi-gifted man this way. He needs a whole array of crutches. Don't weep over your 'one gift' and desire the multi-giftedness of someone else. Rejoice! God looked at you and reasoned you could make it with only one crutch! He took one glance at me growing up and decided I needed all the help I could get!

108   See footnote 51, page 50

It is one thing to travel across the Earth to attend some meetings where the wonderful gifts of the Spirit are being released, but it is quite another thing to immediately announce the superiority or the special quality of the person through whom these gifts are being manifest. That is little short of the adoration of the 'Blessed Saints' and the setting up of shrines in their name!

Our generation has been enormously blessed by some extraordinary outpourings of the Holy Spirit, and I have enjoyed my share of journeys to sit at the well-springs that have so wonderfully re-sourced the Body of Christ in our day. I have been part of the crowds that flocked to the outpouring. Jesus knew full well that crowds don't always show up for the right reasons. Neither did they all leave with an accurate picture of what happened and why. Some just gather to see the signs. Jesus once said: "This is a wicked generation. It asks for a miraculous sign, but none will be given it except the sign of Jonah." [109]

One such crowd gathered, night after night, and one name above all others began to be recognized for his 'special anointing' - the gifted one. The media gave full coverage. All around the world people watched, even gathering for relayed telecasts. A friend gave me a video to view at home. It was a Thursday morning. I was alone, so I turned on the video player and slid in the cassette. It took only a few minutes before I started to cry. What was the matter with me? Was I so moved by the roar of the crowd or the shouts of the preacher? No. The tears were wrung out of me because if I had not cried I felt I would have been physically sick. Something was so wrong about what I was watching. To testify to these misgivings, however, put me out of step with just about everyone around me. Was I that unspiritual to think the latest 'move of God' was somehow hollow?

It was some months later it before it became clear to everyone that there were obvious gifts involved in the meetings but a terrible absence of godly character.

109   Luke 11:29 NIV

Years before I had addressed this when I wrote a song called 'Fall Upon Us'.

> I get so tired of religion, I never did like compromise,
> I wasn't born to go to meetings in a Charismatic paradise.
> Our worship should be more than singing
> with one or two hands slightly raised.
> The bottom line of our ministries is;
> 'Who really gets the praise?'
>
> And if we minister with signs following, isn't it up to us to find
> How to lay hold of the holiness that the signs follow behind?
> You see the giftings of the Spirit were not simply meant to meet
> The selfish needs of a Christian; t
> he gifts were given for the street.
>
> What will this age become known for?
> How will they view us from beyond?
> We've had the greatest revelation;
> the question is: did we respond?
> They will not count up all our meetings
> and ask us how much it all cost.
> They'll simply look at us and question:
> "Did you ever touch the lost"? [110]

'The Gifts were given for the street'. I don't think we've got that one yet. It does not seem to occur to many of us that every activity associated with the Church, be it the fellowship, the worship, our relationship with God and our love for His Word, would all be better served in Heaven. There is, then, only one good reason for us to remain here on Earth – the lost. And yet still we concentrate the vast majority of our efforts on the other things, even to the point where we assume that the Gifts of The Spirit were given for our entertainment, edification, comfort and enjoyment.

---

110   'Fall Upon Us' by Bill Davidson, from the album 'Not For Lazy Listeners'
       – © 1990.

When Jesus promised that the power of the Holy Spirit would fall upon us, He also told us what the consequence would be. He did not say "And when the Holy Spirit has come upon you, you will have much better meetings, much more fun at the altar, and my Gifts will be released just after the preaching is over, that is if the pastor has time to preach because the worship will go on for ever"!

He actually said: "But you will receive power when the Holy Spirit comes on you; and you will be my witnesses in Jerusalem, and in all Judea and Samaria, and to the ends of the earth." [111]

From the very birth of the Church, the manifestations of the Gifts of the Spirit were welcome in gatherings of believers and should be to this day, but have you considered their workings in the office, or in the supermarket? Remember, the first signs of church growth took place on a street.

The Gifts are simply manifestations of Jesus, and He regularly expressed Himself in some ungodly places to some very ungodly people. He didn't seem to have to wait for an altar call in order to get the gifts going. He sat by a well or at a party, or even in a bar, and He was Himself.

When Jesus spoke to the woman at the well, He manifested the Gift of Knowledge, The Word of Wisdom and several other things which would later be released to the whole Church after the resurrection. Take a look at the wonderful story. It is so touching.

The woman may be assumed to have led an immoral life for some years. Some suggest that having come to the well at Noon, [112] she was avoiding contact with other women who probably shunned her. She was skilled at winning men. Within seconds, she knew how to engage them in conversation that went to the heart of their interests. To catch

---

111   Acts 1:8 NIV
112   John 4:6 'It was about the sixth hour.' NIV Nine o'clock 'the third hour' (Acts 2:15)

a contemporary Christian man she would have to have watched a lot of ESPN to know how to engage his interests. With Jesus she probed to see where His interests lay. Jesus would have none of it. He said: "Go and call your husband and come back here." [113]

This was evidence of what we call a 'Word of Knowledge', [114] and it went right to the heart of the matter and straight to the heart of the woman. She admitted: "I have no husband." Perhaps she thought this would attract this fine young man even more, and she still had some impressive things to say to him about comparative theology! [115] But Jesus was seeing through her, literally.

"You are right when you say you have no husband.
The fact is, you have had five husbands, and the man you now have is not your husband. What you have just said is quite true." [116]

She was impressed, to say the least. She recognized his prophetic ability – yet another Gift of the Spirit being manifested. But something was happening in her as she was being uncovered in this way. I use that term discretely. She was being uncovered, but not in the perverse ways that other men had treated her. Jesus was uncovering her sin – and yet she did not feel threatened by Him. The final verses of this story see her running to the town and shouting to the people, "Come, see a man who told me everything I ever did." [117]

This is remarkable! Find someone who has just been 'stripped bare' by truth, and you usually find someone running for cover. But there was something in Jesus that revealed herself to herself, and yet left her feeling secure.

Our tendency is always to hide our sin. The idea of our private vanities and sinfulness being revealed to the world is frightening.

113   John 4:16 NIV
114   1 Corinthians 12:8 NKJV
115   John 4:20
116   John 4:17,18 NIV
117   Jon 4:29 NIV

Have you ever worried about getting close to people with a prophetic edge on their lives, just in case something might be revealed which you would rather keep secret? But Jesus revealed it all, and she felt safer and better for it. That is because Jesus was not just the personal manifestation of what we call the Gifts, He was also the full expression of what we call the Fruits. His ability to discern and open up evil wherever He saw it is beyond doubt. The people followed Him not only for the signs, but also for the sheer beauty of His personality – His character – the beauty of Jesus.

John describes Jesus as being "full of grace and truth". [118] Do you notice the perfect balance there? If you show grace without truth, you create deception. If you tell the truth without grace, you sow destruction. Jesus walked in perfect maturity. Another word for that is 'balance'.

Walking is simply the maintenance of balance between extremes – left, right, left, right. It's the same with maturity. Jesus walked with grace and truth perfectly balanced. That's how we must walk in the balance of our Gifts and our Character. Neither one denies nor weakens the other, but without the other, either one is dangerous and potentially destructive.

The Bible says: 'But to each one of us grace has been given as Christ apportioned it. This is why it says: "When he ascended on high, he led captives in his train and gave gifts to men." ' [119] In the moment of His ascension He was releasing Himself back to His Church, and spreading Himself around. What was once the ability of Jesus is now released through the Gifts of The Spirit. But woe to the man who handles the gift without the character of the Giver! It takes real character to pick up your crutch.

---

118   John 1:14
119   Ephesians 4:7,8

11

And in the End...Success

In the 1980s, I wrote a song that started: "I don't want to die with my music still in me". [120] Now, twenty-something years later and closing in on fifty years of ministry, I still feel the same. There's a lot of 'music' still in there. Some of it is actual music, the songs I churn out fairly frequently, more geared to worship now than the cutting prophetic stuff of past decades. The other 'music' still inside is the deposit of things I still want to do, things still undone, even things not yet imagined.

I haven't yet come to the place where I feel I have no more to give - thank God - and yet I am of the age which would have been marked by retirement back in my old denomination. As I write, a reunion of my college class is taking place over in England. In the early 1960s, I was the second youngest among them. It would have been interesting to see them all again, but I am not sure why! No doubt comparisons could have been made. We'd check each other out and become suitably impressed or maybe somewhat

---

120   'I Don't Want to Die' by Bill Davidson, from the album 'Not For Lazy Listeners'

depressed by the results. There will be people there this week who will be recognized as conspicuously successful and others, I suppose, who will feel that their lives have been unspectacular.

My life has been a vivid example of what success really is, and what it is not. From time to time, I have described my life as having been lived out 'backwards'. I started off with big crowds, acclaim, thousands - even millions of ready listeners, and all of that while still in my teens. Then, over the years, while I can still enjoy large crowds from time to time, my ministry – even my life in general – is smaller, more intimate, and yet infinitely more successful.

Mention 'The Mall' to average Americans, and they picture a plastic bio-sphere inside which Old Navy, J.C. Penney's and Target rule in a haven for credit cards. To a Londoner however, The Mall holds a little more sophistication. It is a mile-long highway that runs from Trafalgar Square, through Admiralty Arch, passing Horse Guards Parade on the left and the Institute of Contemporary Arts to your right. St James Park continues leftward while the top right hand corner is adorned by Clarence House, which sits in secondary splendor to the piece of real estate at the end, past the Victoria Memorial: Buckingham Palace. This is the residence of the reigning Royal Family – that is, when they aren't visiting my birthplace of Aberdeenshire, in Scotland.

Onto this hallowed mile, I steered our not so trusty Renault Dauphine. A Rolls Royce glided noiselessly in front of us and several Bentleys behind. It was 1967 and The Joystrings, Britain's first contemporary Christian music group, were being honored by a visit to 'Buck House' for the Queen's Garden Party. Along with the group; Joy Webb, Peter and Sylvia Dalziel, Wycliffe Noble and me, Wycliffe's wife Elizabeth and my fiancé Jean were both invited.

It was Jean's meager college grant that funded our investment into this wonder of French engineering in which we now approached the Royal domain. Our little Renault was our first car. It didn't last long – not even until we were married the next year, which had something to do with its age, but also related to the fact that at that time I didn't even know we were supposed to replenish the oil as well as the petrol.

We called the car "Nippy", a name more hopeful than descriptive. When we asked it to nip around town it invariably sputtered to a halt. During that era, the French automobile industry seemed to believe that a car's suspension should mimic the feel of a drunken kangaroo trying to make its way through rush hour traffic. All in all, it was quite an exciting vehicle, and all we could afford.

Inch by inch we made it up The Mall, hoping and praying we wouldn't end up stalling at the Palace gates and be seen pushing our vehicle ignominiously out of the way while other more reputable vehicles made their stately way past. More than one policeman gazed in disbelief as our little blue rowing boat bobbed along in the wake of the big black battleships ahead and astern.

We were directed to a parking area to the left of the Victoria Monument. Thankfully, we had arrived without incident. What happened on the way home didn't matter. We had made it to the Queen's house! We had picked up Joy Webb along the way, and as we walked toward the main gate we were joined by the rest of The Joystrings. This was going to be fun. At least we'd see inside the Palace grounds and, who knows, we might even catch a glimpse of the Queen herself.

A group of photographers stood around the gate and one of them shouted "Here they are!" and they began running towards us. We all turned to look behind us to see which international dignitary they were referring to, but no-one was there. Then it dawned on us. We were "they" and the cameras clicked merrily as we walked into the grounds of Buckingham Palace.

Once inside the gates we were processed through security, which in those days was no more than a quick glance at our official invitations. They were beautiful invitations with the Royal Coat of Arms embossed at the top and our names hand-written in perfect copperplate. "Her Majesty Requests The Pleasure…" At least that's what I recalled about my invitation, because in the meantime I had lost it! This appeared to be no great problem as it seemed that we were expected.

I was quickly whisked off into the Palace itself where some files were checked, and I was released on my own cognizance to find my way through a labyrinth of corridors to join the rest of the group. This gave me an opportunity of which I took full advantage by opening a few doors to explore the rooms along the way. I walked in the general direction of the courtyard which stands in the middle of the four-square building, which is not the solid block it appears to be from the front elevation seen by the general population.

Within minutes, I was back with the group. We walked across the central quadrangle and out through the back block to the wide doors which lead into the gardens at the rear. The Queen's back yard!

Another bonus awaited us as we met with our sponsor, a Member of Parliament who was also a Member of The Royal Household. This doesn't mean, as it sounds, that he sat down for tea with Her Majesty or watched TV with her each night in his slippers. It simply meant he had responsibilities, other than his political position, in the general running of what The Duke of Edinburgh once called 'The Family Business'.

The MP told us we should meet him back in a certain spot just before 3:00pm. We all supposed that this would mean that he had saved us a place where we would have a good view as Her Majesty walked in the gardens and spoke to the Ambassadors and other officials who had gathered for the occasion. Thousands of others, mayors, politicians, overseas dignitaries and the like were also invited, so a good position to see the whole thing was a definite advantage.

Until the designated time, we were determined to make the most of our visit behind the walls of The Palace. This kind of opportunity does not come along too often. We were pleased to see snacks were being served in a large pavilion; mostly minute sandwiches, small enough, one supposed, that if one should happen upon someone famous and one was engaged in conversation, one could swallow one's mouthful and one could make a good impression – without talking with one's mouth full in the process!

I filled my plate and took an iced coffee. At least I think it was iced. Perhaps it had just gone cold! I balanced my plate and a cup in one hand and left my other one free for shaking hands with the rich and famous. (One's right hand should always remain free in case one... OK... we've already done the Royal-speak).

Two steps away from the table my grip on my plate and cup gave way, tipping my iced coffee into the saucer and then onto my plate, turning my Palace goodies into a royal soup. I quickly returned and laid my disaster on the table, deftly getting another cup and plate before anyone noticed. Then the Lord of Somewhere-or-other walked up to the table to be served and stood directly in front of my soupy mess. The butler behind the table looked at him, looked down at my mess, back up at Lord So-and-so and gave him the kind of withering look that only a British under-servant would get away with in the presence of a member of the aristocracy! I didn't own up. I just looked at his Lordship with similar disdain!

Off we went to explore the Palace grounds. Two detachments of Guards' Bands were arrayed in two separate pavilions about thirty yards apart on the main lawn. Each band had its own flag pole on which a standard was hoisted to indicate that they were about to start a piece of music. At the conclusion of the piece, the soldier who was on flag duty (perhaps he had failed at cornet) lowered the flag, seemingly as a signal to the boys a few yards away that it was their turn. Dutifully, the man on flag duty at the other pavilion raised their standard, and the second band began to play. We watched this little ritual take place several times, which had obviously been enacted by similar military groups for centuries before. We wondered if anyone would one day dare to break with tradition and just wink over at the other band, or give them a thumbs-up and shout: "Alright, Jim, your turn!" But no! This was England and on the Palace lawn at least, nothing changeth here!

At three o'clock we arrived back at our designated spot only to find it occupied by a couple of hundred gentlemen, top hats in place, standing beside their ladies with hats the size of small tables. There was no way we could get so much as a glimpse of the action from back there. We were marooned on the tenth row. Oh well, the iced coffee had been good.

At that point, we became aware of someone jumping up and down in front of our section of the crowd. It was our MP – beckoning us to the front. Slowly, disgruntled aristocrats, unused to being told where to stand (or anything else, for that matter) made room for this odd little group of youngsters dressed in Salvation Army uniform. As we arrived at the front row of the crowd we noticed that an avenue had been cleared between our part of the crowd and the hundreds of similarly elegant couples across the way. Yeoman of the Guard [121] in their ceremonial costumes and tall Pike Staffs stood every twenty yards, marking the avenue down which we supposed the Queen would walk. What a treat, we were on the front row!

---

121   The guards at the Tower of London are called **Yeoman Warders or Beefeaters**. In principle they are responsible for looking after any prisoners at the Tower and safeguarding the British crown jewels but they often appear at State functions.

"What are we doing?" we asked, as he separated us from the front row of the onlookers and bade us stand in the middle of the open avenue between the crowds. "Just stand here" he said, before disappearing towards the palace, "and Her Majesty will be along in a minute."

Something solid stirred in my stomach, and it wasn't the iced coffee! Did we hear him right? Did he not say that The Queen would be along shortly? Did someone fail to mention this tiny detail, that in the midst of these thousands of celebrities, politicians and visiting dignitaries, we were the ones about to be presented to The Queen?

Now, crowds were no problem to us. We had lived among masses of people every day of our lives for the previous four years. Our concerts, travels, TV programs, even the odd game of beach soccer, attracted a crowd of onlookers. There was not one person, be they Lord, Lady, Ambassador, President or Prince, who would give us a moment's difficulty. But to British people there is something rather special about meeting the little lady whose face adorns the postage stamp. This side of the Second Coming it's the closest one gets to genuine awe!

Before long a small group appeared at the double doors of the Palace and arranged themselves on the stone steps beyond. The two bands struck up The National Anthem. Hats were doffed. Soldiers saluted and there they were: Her Majesty Queen Elizabeth II and her Prince Consort, His Royal Highness, The Duke of Edinburgh. Their marriage had helped heal the wounds of post-war Britain and The Queen's Coronation had been the reason most of us invested in our first tiny television sets. Every Christmas Day the entire nation would stop whatever festivities they were enjoying, to listen to The Queen's Speech. And now, here we were, looking – albeit from a distance – at the real thing.

The Anthem concluded with a flourish and one of the bands, having duly raised its little standard, burst into "The Hills are Alive with the Sound of Music". The Queen's party began walking down the corridor in the middle of which we stood. And there she was, this tiny lady, the walking postage stamp, the actual "Heads" on the other side of "Tails".

Her party was led by The Lord High Chamberlain. It was seemingly his job to introduce Her Majesty to the selected guests, but it soon became clear that His Lordship's afternoon had already been peppered with one too many tipples of Port. He looked at us, uncertainly, through blood-shot bleary eyes, rather like a Bull Dog eyeing a team of Greyhounds. "A Group from Headquarters, Ma'am," he mumbled. From Queen Victoria's time to that day, 'Headquarters' referred to 101 Queen Victoria Street, London E.C.1., the beloved address of The Salvation Army's International and National Headquarters.

"Oh" she said, in that one-and-only voice, which is unquestionably the sound of The Queen's English, "The Joystrings!" She beamed at us and launched into a twenty minute conversation which assured us that we were not only talking to the Queen, but also a loving Mum, who probably watched our weekly TV shows on Sunday evenings with the family.

The next day most of the national daily newspapers held the story. The Daily Mail splashed a large photo across its front page. The headline read: "The Queen Meets The Joystrings."

The evening before, after our time with Her Majesty was over; we basked in the luminous glow of the event. Her Majesty was (and still is) a charming conversationalist. She has the ability to include everyone in the moment, and she proved to be light hearted and quite a wit. She was interested in the fact that we visited some of the largest prisons to hold concerts in front of hardened criminals. "Oh yes," she said, "the Archbishop of Canterbury says he always likes speaking in prisons. It assures him of a captive audience!" Although we'd heard the Archbishop's line many times before, we laughed heartily! When the Queen tells a joke, you laugh for the simple pleasure of the moment.

The Daily Mail photo caught her, just as I was finishing my attempt at a joke, also on the subject of the inmates of Her Majesty's Prison Service. Being in prison in Britain is described officially as "Detained at Her Majesty's Pleasure". I assured Her Majesty that we went into prisons to help make "Her Majesty's Pleasure" a little more pleasurable. She seemed to get it, as the photo shows.

As she walked away from us, an aristocratic voice from the crowd said: "Charming, quite charming!" We agreed.

Nippy seemed to sense our satisfaction as I drove Jean back to the William Booth College through London's south-east suburbs. The little car must have felt something akin to the emotion enjoyed by the pumpkin with Cinderella aboard. We were silent as we rode. No more needed to be said. We had truly arrived. We had made it. From the funny little group clanging its way through our opening chords and charging blindly into the British Pop Charts earlier in the decade, we were now an excellent concert band, touring throughout Europe and Scandinavia. We filled the largest concert halls in the capital cities wherever we went. But, today, we had been received in Buckingham Palace. We were no longer just a group, but in our own little way we were becoming an institution.

So, that's how my life and ministry started - at the top - an unquestioned success. The only question which remained was "Where do you go from here?" Staying within The Salvation Army might have built on that early foundation. It is an organization in which rank, promotion, publicity and notoriety can help one's ministry career. But that was not to be our future. Where would success come from? How would I even define the term in years to come? The last thing I wanted to be was to end my days singing the songs of The Sixties to aging and retired Salvationists in a vane attempt to recall 'the good old days'! But where do you go after starting at the top?

Fast forward to a mountain overlooking the sprawling city of Bogotá, Colombia; it's the early 1980s. Our Church up in the mountains of New York was growing and reaching out in missions. Colombia had opened up to us, and I knew God was asking us to plant a church, not in the rich north of Colombia's capital city. Not even in the hard working-class areas of the south, but on the muddy hills where the 'Invaciones' clung to the mountainsides. These 'invasions' were nothing more than squatter shanty towns where people who had been displaced from their rural homes by terrorist activities now sought shelter and a new life in the lie that belongs on the streets of every major city, which are never paved with gold!

A few local people sat around me. We had gathered to share with them the idea of starting a Church right there in barrio Los Olivos. A woman had opened her home to us for the occasion. It comprised of three pieces of corrugated metal sheeting, leaning together for mutual support. I'm not sure what the roof consisted of, but the door was triangular because it was simply the space between two of the walls which leaned towards one another. The floor was the ground. It had been raining – which in Bogotá was no great surprise – and as it ran down the hill toward the city streets below, the rainwater mingled with the filth of everyday poverty. I wore the evidence on the seat of my jeans. There were no chairs, but as I sat there in the slimy mud I was so elated, so excited. We were planting a church – The Church – and I felt I was experiencing success.

Back in the Sixties I received an invitation to attend a service in Westminster Cathedral, the headquarters of Catholicism in Britain. I didn't know what it was all about, but it came from the Headmaster of a Catholic school I had recently visited where I had sung and shared Jesus with the boys. It was a weeknight in the evening. I donned my Joystrings uniform – light grey rather than the traditional dark blue, as it was better for the TV cameras. I recall wearing a pair of suede Hush Puppies (definitely not regulation) as I drove our Austin Mini into town.

I was told to arrive at the back door of the Cathedral where a gentleman in a long lacy robe greeted me and ushered me inside. "If you want to change, this is the robing room" he said. "No thanks, I'm fine as I am" I replied. He smiled and opened the door to a large room where about fifty elderly gentlemen were in various stages of 'robing'. It didn't take me long to realize I was a little out of place.

I was introduced to Arch Bishops, Bishops and Canons (and I wasn't even a toy gun)! We were then assembled into a long line, two abreast. There were two men in front, an Arch Bishop and a mere Bishop. The head of the Methodist Church stood behind them with me next to him. "Well done, Salvation Army," I thought. "Third in line."

I was sure that any minute someone would realize the mistake and drag me out of the line-up. I tried a little humor. "All we need now is Cardinal Heenan," I quipped to my parade buddy, the Methodist Bishop. He smiled, inquiringly, but before I could explain, the door opened and in walked none other than the Cardinal himself. "Maybe I should have tried for the Pope," I thought – to myself.

It was an administrative blunder of course. When I informed the Army's Headquarters about my night out in Westminster, they scolded me. "You should have forwarded the invitation to the General, or at least the Chief of The Staff", I was informed. I had already realized that! I duly informed the Headmaster of the faux pas and told him that the invitation should have been sent to the head of The Salvation Army. "But I thought that was you!" He replied. I thought better of passing on that little morsel to Headquarters.

The climax of the evening had been when we began a processional from a side door beside the High Altar, down the left wing of the massive Cathedral, which was packed to the walls with what looked like a couple of thousand people, and then back down the central aisle, at the end of which several large thrones were arranged and – sure enough – young Billy was conducted to his throne, among all the aged ecclesiastical luminaries! After a quick look at the Order of Service I satisfied myself that I was nowhere to be seen on the menu, so I settled back for the fun of it. "Jean will never believe this one," I thought.

But let me tell you something. I would not take a thousand thrones in Westminster in exchange for one seat in the mud of Los Olivos. Success, I have learned, is obedience; the sort of obedience that lands you in the right place, at the right time, doing the right thing. Success is not found in the acclaim of the majority, it is discovered somewhere in a lovingly obedient response to an audience of One.

Our little meeting in a broken down excuse for a home on that Colombian mountainside gave no hint of what lay ahead. A few years later Wendy Luff, from Plymouth in England, made her way to Bogotá accompanied by Barbara Brown, my church secretary. Barbara went for "a year". That was in the early in the 1990s, and she's been there along side Pastora Wendy, ever since.

Wendy and Barbara have faithfully served the community of Barrio Los Olivos, paying for the education of well over a thousand children, bringing healing to the relationships of countless broken 'units' (there have been very few, if any, whole families). Now Iglesia Oasis stands firm on the hillside of the community which has grown out of the curse of the Invasions into a recognized City Barrio.

Out of an illiterate crowd Wendy and Barbara have trained up a literate, educated community. By the life-giving power of the Holy

Spirit, these two heroes of the faith have used God's creative ways to transform broken, down-cast lives. They often organize game nights, involving children and adults alike, which model positive aspects of life. Wendy once told me "We even had to teach them how to smile". Few had ever played games as children. It was not uncommon for a child to be tied to a bed or a chair all day while her mother went down to the city streets to beg, or worse. Through her ministry and the Fundación La Esperanza [122] Wendy has even seen 'our kids' go off to University. The first of 'their people' to do so.

I used to have this conversation with God. I asked Him if we could possibly be sent to an easy field of endeavor, just now and again. Maybe some people in the Bahamas needed some encouragement. Don't the rich need a pastor!? I've mingled with the greats of our time enough to know it wouldn't turn my head to enjoy a little luxury along the way.

I sense His smile and together we laugh at the thought. He knows that I am determined to be a success, so consequently I'll just go where he sends me, and so far, that hasn't been back to the Palace, or to the 'big names' in show business I once knew, or to the wealthy or aristocratic.

When I think of that throne in Westminster Cathedral, I am reminded of the only other throne I sit on these days. One of my regular haunts is to visit the West African city of Monrovia, Liberia. That nation has been ravaged by civil war but is now healing its wounds. Liberians have nothing. Few have a job, running water, electricity or decent food, but they are bright, intelligent, inventive and optimistic. My main friend there is Pastor Philipson Nagbe [123] and whenever I visit his church, he insists I sit on a large wooden

---

122 The Esperanza Foundation – once a children's home in the country, now a non-residential city ministry based in Los Olivos and elsewhere in Bogotá

123 Philipson Nagbe – pronounced 'Nam-weh' – Pastor of Liberian Christian Evangelical Church, Monrovia, Liberia.

throne, complete with a small foot stool. In Monrovia, it's a sign of respect and honor. To me, however, it's a cause of embarrassment as I sit, drenched in sweat, enthroned, but in somewhat different circumstances to my Westminster days.

My 'backwards' progress in the eyes of the world was clear when I last visited Paris. I was driving a fifteen seater van through the middle of the city. If you think that's an achievement, Jean was driving another fifteen-seater directly behind me, doing a great job at following me through the city center — and Parisian drivers make Manhattan look like Sunday School! Our passengers were young students from The King's School in Lake Luzerne. [124]

We drove along Le place de l'Hôtel de Ville and past the government house of that remarkable city. "That's the Hotel de Ville" I said. "The City Hall of Paris". The students were mildly interested, until someone spotted a dog, or a car (or a young lady) that demanded more attention.

So, here I was, driving kids close by a building to which, in 1966, The Joystrings had been driven, direct from Le Gare du Nord railway station, for a welcoming reception with the Mayor of Paris and a national press conference. Back then, you see, I was a "success".

I didn't pass on that information to my student passengers. I had an overwhelming feeling it would sound like some old guy reflecting on "the good old days". But, again, that would not be the case. My driving seat that day, with the great young people of The King's School beside me, was the place of success for me at that time in my life. Who really cares if no-one else knew we were there and no-one from the Press corps would give us a second glance?

Soon we were gliding along the Avenue des Champs-Élysées. I looked over at the building which had once housed "Le Top Ten"

124   See: http://kingsschool.info

club where we had headlined 'back in the day'. Again I refrained from reporting it to my contemporary charges.

What a fascinating life – even if it has been backwards in its progress in the eyes of the world. It reminds me of how the Early Church was once described as "These that have turned the world upside down". [125] The fact is, they were turning a world which was already upside down, the right way up!

What the world sees as the marks of success are often the roots or the fruits of failure. Jesus said: "Woe to you when all men speak well of you, for that is how their fathers treated the false prophets." [126]

Somewhere along the line of life most of us begin to wonder how we will be remembered. It would be so much more convenient if we could write our own epitaph. My fellow countryman, Andrew Carnegie, did just that, although it was suitably self effacing: "A Man Who Knew How to Enlist in His Service Better Men than Himself."

As for me, I'd like to share David's epitaph. It wouldn't take much of a headstone to house it. Luke recorded it in the Acts of the Apostles. He wrote: "David, after he had served the purposes of God in his generation, fell asleep." [127]

I notice that David served God's purposes in *his* generation before passing away. I think that has been my constant position. I have always believed that eternal truths and the way they are communicated should be relevant to the present day, simply because that's what makes them eternal – their consistent relevance.

Some powerful forces will tempt even the sincerest of souls to settle in the security of the status quo. True success, however, lies just

125   Acts 17:6 KJV
126   Luke 6:26 NIV
127   Acts 13:36 NAS

beyond the next horizon. Why should it not? How can people who were created to live for ever, settle in any one time and place? So the next horizon it is, and only obedience will get us there.

A man's epitaph is the summary of the marks God left upon his life when meeting up with him along the way. And whether or not my marks look good to others, I cherish them, "For if you possess these qualities in increasing measure, they will keep you from being ineffective and unproductive" [128]

Yours, marked for life.....

---

128   2 Peter 1:8 NIV

LaVergne, TN USA
04 February 2010
172155LV00003B/27/P